COLLECTING QUALITATIVE DATA USING DIGITAL METHODS

for BUSINESS *and* MANAGEMENT STUDENTS

Sara Miller McCune founded SAGE Publishing in 1965 to support the dissemination of usable knowledge and educate a global community. SAGE publishes more than 1000 journals and over 800 new books each year, spanning a wide range of subject areas. Our growing selection of library products includes archives, data, case studies and video. SAGE remains majority owned by our founder and after her lifetime will become owned by a charitable trust that secures the company's continued independence.

Los Angeles | London | New Delhi | Singapore | Washington DC | Melbourne

COLLECTING QUALITATIVE DATA USING DIGITAL METHODS

for BUSINESS and MANAGEMENT STUDENTS

REBECCA WHITING &
KATRINA PRITCHARD

Los Angeles | London | New Delhi
Singapore | Washington DC | Melbourne

Los Angeles | London | New Delhi
Singapore | Washington DC | Melbourne

SAGE Publications Ltd
1 Oliver's Yard
55 City Road
London EC1Y 1SP

SAGE Publications Inc.
2455 Teller Road
Thousand Oaks, California 91320

SAGE Publications India Pvt Ltd
B 1/I 1 Mohan Cooperative Industrial Area
Mathura Road
New Delhi 110 044

SAGE Publications Asia-Pacific Pte Ltd
3 Church Street
#10-04 Samsung Hub
Singapore 049483

Editor: Ruth Stitt
Assistant editor: Jessica Moran
Production editor: Sarah Cooke
Copyeditor: Gemma Marren
Proofreader: Christine Bitten
Indexer: Judith Lavender
Marketing manager: Abigail Sparks
Cover design: Francis Kenney
Typeset by: C&M Digitals (P) Ltd, Chennai, India
Printed in the UK

Library of Congress Control Number: 2020945707

British Library Cataloguing in Publication data

A catalogue record for this book is available from the British Library

ISBN 978-1-5264-8993-7
ISBN 978-1-5264-8992-0 (pbk)

At SAGE we take sustainability seriously. Most of our products are printed in the UK using responsibly sourced papers and boards. When we print overseas we ensure sustainable papers are used as measured by the PREPS grading system. We undertake an annual audit to monitor our sustainability.

CONTENTS

LIST OF FIGURES AND TABLES

FIGURES

TABLES

ACKNOWLEDGEMENTS

This book has been inspired by the work (the Age at Work project) that we started together nearly a decade ago when we were both working at Birkbeck, University of London. The project was made possible through funding that Katrina was awarded by the Richard Benjamin Trust; later we received follow-on funding from the School of Business, Economics & Informatics at Birkbeck.

Katrina and Rebecca would like to acknowledge that many excellent colleagues and collaborators have inspired and supported their methodological journey during this time, including:

Dr Chris Carter
Dr Sarah Glozer
Professor Chris Hine
Dr Kate Mackenzie-Davey
Dr Maggie Miller
Dr Cara Reed
Dr Gabrielle Samuel
Professor Gillian Symon

They would also like to thank their PhD students for constantly challenging and questioning methodological issues: Christine, Helen C, Paula, Roger, Helen W and Samantha.

Katrina would also like to dedicate this book to Bill, Jess, Charles and Adam. In loving memory of Sadie, Lola and Freddie who always gave paws for thought.

Rebecca would like to dedicate this book to Raúl in grateful thanks for his support, encouragement and sense of perspective on all matters academic and otherwise.

ABOUT THE AUTHORS

Rebecca Whiting is a Senior Lecturer in the Department of Organizational Psychology at Birkbeck, University of London where she leads the Department's Qualitative Research Group. She is interested in a wide range of qualitative methodologies, including the use of digital and visual data, and in the ethics of conducting research that uses such data. She has published journal articles and book chapters on aspects of qualitative methods, including in *The SAGE Handbook of Qualitative Business and Management Research Methods* and the Oxford University Press volume, *Unconventional Methodology in Organization and Management Research*. Her research topics include the discursive construction of work identities, work-life boundaries, diversity (particularly age, gender and class and how they are socially constructed) and invisible work.

Katrina Pritchard is a Professor in the School of Management, Swansea University. She has published journal articles and book chapters on aspects of qualitative methods, including in *The SAGE Handbook of Qualitative Business and Management Research Methods* and Symon and Cassell's *Qualitative Organizational Research: Core Methods and Current Challenges* (2012). Katrina's methodological interests extend from traditional to creative qualitative methods, including visual and object-based, in addition to digital methods. She researches a range of topics related to issues of identity at work.

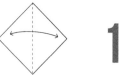

1

INTRODUCTION

The use of **digital methods** is an increasingly important tool for qualitative research. When we talk about using digital methods to collect qualitative data, we are referring to relatively new techniques within business and management research made possible by the arrival of contemporary communication technologies. Like interviews (Cassell, 2015), digital methods can be used to investigate a wide range of topics, within different research paradigms, and produce data that can be analysed using various methods. However, whereas interviews are well-established methods of data collection, these technology-enabled approaches are much less developed in terms of what they are, when and where they can be used and how to carry them out. Students, and potentially the academic staff who supervise their projects or handle their ethics applications, may therefore be less familiar with digital methods. Although these may involve using some of the same proprietary tools such as specific Internet browsers that we encounter in our everyday lives, it is important to distinguish these methods from the more general and familiar activity of Internet browsing for information about a topic. Collecting qualitative Internet data using digital methods is a systematic technique involving many of the same steps as any other research methodology and with the aim of producing data which – through analysis – can be interpreted and used to address a research question.

The aim of this book is therefore to provide an accessible guide to using specific digital methods (ones which use and study web-based activities and settings) for qualitative data collection as part of a Masters level research project in management, organization or business studies. We use these domain terms interchangeably, reflecting our own academic backgrounds and occupational contexts. In this book, we introduce and explain two related approaches we term '**tracking**' and '**trawling**'.

The book addresses the underlying **philosophical assumptions** that inform the uses of these methods, discusses their key components and considers how these may be organized to use the methods. We provide examples of published studies that have used the methods. The book concludes by reflecting on methodological strengths and weaknesses of tracking and trawling, some tips on preparing for data analysis and suggestions for further reading. The focus throughout the book is on applying these methods to the relatively small-scale time-bound research that is characteristic of a Masters research project and how to manage these approaches so that their use results in a deliverable outcome.

The following topics are reviewed in this chapter:

- a brief history of the Internet in research to contextualize these developments
- types of qualitative Internet data
- reflexivity in Internet research
- tracking and trawling and how they can be used and adapted
- our approach to this book, its structure and our assumptions for its use.

A BRIEF HISTORY OF THE INTERNET IN RESEARCH

Since the inception of the Internet as a global system of interconnected computer networks in the late 1980s and early 1990s (Cohen-Almagor, 2011), many aspects of contemporary life have been transformed. In relation to the field of business and management, it is difficult to name a topic or practice not impacted by the Internet. Business and organizational use of the Internet as an everyday tool has significantly changed working practices and introduced new ones. This has opened up the Internet as both location and source of new phenomena; issues of interest to management scholars no longer solely take place within a physical workplace. This presents both challenges and opportunities in terms of what to study and how, as we recognize the potential of 'research not just about the Internet but also on it and through it and constituted within it' (Hine, 2005: 205). Challenges include adapting ethical principles for Internet research and designing Internet research that is achievable. These are, however, set against the very considerable opportunity afforded by the accessibility of new configurations of people, discussions and other materials on almost any topic of interest (Hine, 2012). Indeed, the Internet has been described as 'the most comprehensive electronic archive of written material representing our world and peoples' opinions, concerns, and desires' (Eysenbach and Till, 2001: 1103).

In relation to research, however, it is worth pausing to consider the particular characteristics of the Internet that underpin these opportunities and challenges. Originally conceived as an open and unregulated space, the Internet is not a single unitary location. It contains spaces that its users may conceive of as private even if publicly accessible (Whiting and Pritchard, 2017). It transcends national and linguistic boundaries and is subject to the various policies, laws and governance of different countries (Palfrey, 2010). In terms of human behaviour, however, the Internet still retains a certain Wild West character, for example, with trolling (targeting individuals with controversial, inflammatory and off-topic messages on social media) and malicious software. Those engaging with digital methods may encounter these perils at some stage (we briefly mention our brush with **malware** in Chapter 4). Ethical considerations must therefore examine the risk of harm to potential participants and to researchers whose own digital footprint may make them a target for these activities. Lastly, the multi-modal, dynamic and transitory nature of Internet material (a particular challenge in research) is countered by attempts to capture and stabilize its content through archives such as the **WayBack Machine** and initiatives such as the **UK Web Archive** (UKWA), which collects millions of websites each year. We will return to these Internet characteristics at various points in our discussion of digital methods.

Early digital research in the social sciences started tentatively but soon incorporated varied online and Internet-based approaches (Fielding et al., 2008) covering a 'wide range of activities' (British Psychological Society, 2007: 1) and from a broad range of research orientations. It often involved the (relatively) straightforward transfer of an existing method to the Internet (Hine, 2013). Thus, a paper survey became an online or email survey (Bachmann and Elfrink, 1996); a face-to-face interview was conducted by email, Skype (Janghorban et al., 2014) or instant messaging (Hinchcliffe and Gavin, 2009) and Internet ethnographies applied notions of participant-observation to chat-room communities and other online spaces (Kozinets, 2010). This prompted examination of their acceptability by participants (Thompson et al., 2003), comparison with more traditional methods of data collection (for example, the review of survey approaches by Yun and Trumbo, 2000) and evaluation of their effectiveness (Simsek and Veiga, 2001). Practical considerations were also a concern, reflecting how the application of a specific research method was mediated through both researchers' and participants' engagement with technology. Researchers have also acknowledged the further methodological reorientation required, such as examining the relationship between online and offline activity (Kozinets, 2010).

Another key aspect of early Internet research was the examination of new organizational forms, for example, Rindova and Kotha's (2001) study of web service company **Yahoo**, and new ways of organizing for commercial success through virtual Internet communities (Rothaermel and Sugiyama, 2001). Research also examined companies' web presence, for instance Lemke's (1999) study of the corporate website as a new medium of communication in organizational change. Research engagement with the Internet in the field of management studies and the utilization of online and Internet-based methods was initially comparatively modest (Sproull et al., 2007). The primary analytic focus was on text, as in Coupland and Brown's (2004) analysis of email exchanges posted on an organizational forum. Here, while the dynamic nature of data is acknowledged, the scale and format of the data were comparable with other 'offline' communication studies, an early indication that qualitative Internet research might not seek to emulate the scale of the '**big data**' approach of quantitative studies. More recently, as part of the 'visual' turn in organization and management research (Meyer et al., 2013), attention has extended to Internet images such as Swan's (2017) examination of representations of work femininities on a website offering coaching targeted at women and our own analysis of stock photos of men and women of various ages to unpack the visual construction of gendered ageing at work within online news media (Pritchard and Whiting, 2015). Chapter 5 contains further examples of **visual digital data** in published studies in business and management research.

Early reticence towards digital methods is changing as more researchers in business and management studies engage with the Internet as a source of data and methodological tools. Many of the main journals in this field contain studies where digital methods have been used to collect qualitative Internet data. The scope of work in this area incorporates the use of methods translated for the Internet such as **online ethnography** (Cordoba-Pachon and Loureiro-Koechlin, 2015) as well as analysis of new genres of Internet data such as social media to explore its use by organizations (Glozer et al., 2019; Sundstrom and Levenshus, 2017). In Chapter 5 we introduce examples of published studies that use tracking and trawling methods (either on their own or in combination with other methods) to provide more detailed illustrations of how collecting qualitative digital data has been used in business and management research. We exclude studies that use **netnography** (for example, Kozinets, 2019) or related approaches of online ethnography as these are distinct and well-established methods.

TYPES OF INTERNET DATA

The Internet has enabled and generated both qualitative and quantitative research. The latter is closely associated with the 'big data' approaches mentioned above that produce topographical maps of Internet phenomena, illuminating the overall shape and form of the issues under consideration (Murthy, 2008). The focus of this book is, however, on qualitative research. This is described as 'typically oriented to the inductive study of socially constructed reality, focusing on meanings, ideas and practices, taking the native's point of view seriously' (Alvesson and Deetz, 2000: 1). Qualitative research comprises a wide range of methods developed from a variety of theoretical perspectives and underpinned, particularly within the European context, by a range of different philosophical traditions; their use has helped make visible and acceptable alternatives to positivist approaches (Symon and Cassell, 2016). In Chapter 2 we examine how tracking and trawling methods can be used differently, depending on the broader philosophical orientation of the research project. For now, in the context of Internet research, a key contrast with 'big data' studies is the way in which qualitative research focuses on human/digital interactions as we navigate these maps of online phenomena, examining experiences shaped through and by the Internet. Studies that do so generate qualitative data (non-numeric data that can be textual or visual) as we discuss further in Chapter 5.

As we note above, qualitative Internet data are often **multi-modal**, deploying both **textual** and **visual forms of communication** (Bell and Leonard, 2018; Meyer et al., 2013). Textual and visual modes both contribute meaning but, with their different affordances, each has its own distinctive ways of representing and constructing the world (Kress and van Leeuwen, 1996). These may work independently, such as visuals conveying what cannot be said in writing (Monson et al., 2016) but also work in combination (Meyer et al., 2013; Swan, 2017). Management research has 'rather neglected such interplay of verbal and visual text' (Meyer et al., 2013: 522), prompting calls for methodological approaches that can 'contend with multi-semiotic representations' (Oddo, 2013: 26) and 'integrate and/or contrast these two modes of communication' (Meyer et al., 2013: 522). This undoubtedly represents an opportunity for scholars in this field to conduct research that examines both texts and images. We understand that this may be a challenge for those undertaking a Masters research project given the need to analyse both modes of data and integrate these analyses in presenting the findings. In this book, most of the examples of studies therefore involve either textual or visual data, but in Chapter 5 we examine a broader range of studies including those with more complex research designs than would be anticipated for a Masters research project so that the potential of these methods can be fully appreciated.

REFLEXIVITY IN INTERNET RESEARCH

These studies noted above highlight the need for methods and tools that can be used with Internet data. Not all publications that use qualitative Internet data specify exactly how the data have been selected or collected. Researchers may also deploy different terms to describe similar methods, particularly around digital versions of existing methods. **Digital ethnography** (Murthy, 2008), netnography (Kozinets, 2019) and online ethnography (Cordoba-Pachon and Loureiro-Koechlin, 2015) are all used to describe very similar ways of conducting ethnography online (and which are different from tracking and trawling and beyond the scope of this book). This can make it harder to track the academic literature around a particular digital method. And not all academics have been fully convinced of the Internet's potential contribution to research. For instance, Travers (2009: 172) commented that 'it is hard to see how new technologies add much that is really new to qualitative research … more worryingly they flatter us into thinking that, because the methods are new or innovative, no further thought about methodological issues or how one analyses the data are required'.

Our answer to this, indeed our approach in this book and elsewhere in our work (Pritchard and Whiting, 2012a), has been to use digital methods – and their development – as an opportunity for **reflexivity**. This is defined by Hardy and colleagues (2001: 554) as an 'awareness of the situatedness of scientific knowledge and an understanding of the research and research community from which the knowledge has appeared'. We have applied a reflexive approach to examine the assumptions we have as researchers, such as what constitutes data and participants. One area where our reflexive approach has been particularly relevant is in relation to the ethics of Internet research (Whiting and Pritchard, 2017). Ethics have been a particular focus (Ess, 2009) as researchers (us included) have grappled to make sense of applying existing ethical frameworks to the Internet context. Some of the early debates (Pittenger, 2003) foreshadowed the complexity recognized today, for instance, in determining whether a particular Internet space is public or private and whether those who have generated material within it are human participants for the purposes of ethical considerations. We discuss this in more depth in Chapter 3. For now, we turn to a second area where we have adopted a reflexive approach, namely our development of digital methods.

INTRODUCING TRACKING AND TRAWLING

Tracking and trawling are two related approaches, at either end of a methodological spectrum, and are defined as set out in Table 1.1 below. Very briefly, they use a variety of digital (often proprietary) means to collect selected material from the Internet. For example, a proprietary Internet tool such as the automated **Google Alerts** could be used with the search terms 'age' and 'work' to capture new online UK media that is posted on the web each subsequent day that mention these words. In collecting Internet material in this way, tracking and trawling follow in the tradition of collecting documents and undertaking documentary analysis in business and management research (Lee, 2012), taking this approach online and accommodating the inherent multi-modality of Internet material. This makes it possible to collect a wide range of different types of document not just directly from organizations' websites (annual reports, policies, minutes of meetings), but also from other Internet sources including government, newspapers, courts, campaign groups and new web-enabled genres such as social media. These sources are likely to feature not just texts but images as well. The wide range of material and its multi-modality enable the researcher to develop and address a wide range of research questions.

Table 1.1 Definitions of tracking and trawling

Approach	Description
Tracking	Uses a variety of digital means (such as using proprietary tools) to track (or follow) a particular event and/or people or groups of interest and/or a concept due to their engagement with a specific topic of relevance to the research. It is usually prospective in that it involves tracking from the start of the project onwards in time to capture new material as it is published on the Internet.
Trawling	Uses specific key word search (such as in search engines) to provide potentially relevant material across a variety of source types (e.g. websites, **blogs**, **Twitter**). It is usually retrospective in that it involves trawling the Internet for existing material that has already been published or posted before the start of the research project.

As we noted above, an example of tracking would therefore be for a researcher to set up automated Google Alerts at the start of the project with the search terms 'age' and 'work' to capture any new online UK media as it is posted on the web. If the researcher were to use an Internet browser to search manually for these terms in selected online UK media that had appeared previously in the last two years, this would be an example of trawling.

We developed these methods for a number of reasons. We had designed a research project to examine web-based data on the topic of age at work, which was funded (see our legacy research blog for further details: https://ageatwork.wordpress.com/). We needed to develop a systematic way of identifying and collecting the data and we were interested in developing a methodology that was both practical and promoted 'design transparency' (Karpf, 2012), such as in the writing up of the study for publication. The project itself provided a 'live' context for our discussion of the practical, methodological and ethical issues that we faced. We discussed the features and properties of the Internet that presented us with challenges such as the dynamic and transitory nature of web-based material and the notion of a digital footprint (of ourselves through our blogging and tweeting on the project and of others such as those we subsequently 'tracked' for data). As we mentioned earlier, our approach was to reflect on these challenges and in doing so to situate them within existing methodological debates rather than making any claims that these were new or innovative (Pritchard and Whiting, 2012a). In our early discussions about the project design, we knew that we would want to capture (a) the topics of interest about age at work, (b) the different voices of organizations, groups or individuals engaged and mentioned in these topics, and (c) the digital locations in which all this was taking place. Over time, we came to think of these as the concepts, actors and sources or the 'what', 'who' and 'where' of our research data. We return to this in Chapters 2 and 3 when we discuss research design.

The terms tracking and trawling were coined by us as a result of our reflections on the characteristics of the Internet (Pritchard and Whiting, 2012b). We made natural world metaphorical comparisons between seeking data on the World Wide Web and hunting on land (tracking) and fishing at sea (trawling). At an elementary level, tracking for us involved a sense of following a target that was moving forwards in new and unpredictable directions; trawling encompassed a sense of seeking what was already there and was waiting to be retrieved. We originally conceived of these as two quite separate digital methods representing opposite points on a spectrum in terms of Internet data collection. Over time, as we have used, developed and reflected on these methods, we have come to see that tracking and trawling are not quite as distinct or discrete as we first thought (see Table 1.2). A project might readily involve a combination of the two. This was the case with the data for our paper on reconstructing retirement (Whiting and Pritchard, 2020). We used Google Alerts with piloted search terms to generate returns which we reviewed for relevance as new material appeared on the web each day (tracking). The particular focus for this paper was online media coverage of an insurance company report which introduced the acronym WEARY to represent the 'working entrepreneurial active retiree' (too poor to retire, too old to get a job hence retirement needing to be a time of entrepreneurial endeavour). We selected and collated all relevant material which was linked to in the alerts that related to this report. We then switched to trawling. This involved two aspects: first, using a **snowballing technique**, we followed promising links in data we had collected via our tracking method and second, we searched online using a web browser to locate any other material that mentioned the report in UK online media. Again, we selected and collated all further relevant material to ensure that we had not missed anything. The combined material from both tracking and trawling was our dataset for this paper (we discuss this a little further in Chapter 5).

This example shows the adaptability of tracking and trawling and how they can be used in combination. A researcher might start with tracking and then funnel down into trawling. Although the methods share certain common features as set out in Table 1.2, one of the key differences between them is their relationship with time. We think it likely that, for most Masters research projects, students will undertake trawling where the emphasis is on identifying material that has already been posted on the Internet. Tracking – with its prospective focus on identifying material as and when it is posted online – is more appropriate for larger research studies carried out over a longer period of time. However, Masters research students could feasibly opt to use a small-scale tracking project related to a specific event, as we discuss further in Chapter 4.

Table 1.2   Features of tracking and trawling

Tracking	Trawling
	Differences
Automated search, usually set up to repeat over time	Manual one-off search
Prospective in time	Retrospective in time
Researcher cannot add new search terms retrospectively, only prospectively	Researcher can add new search terms or platforms to do a manual retrospective search at any stage
	Similarities
Require researcher to develop key search terms	
Can use proprietary tools	
Can be combined with other methods of data collection	
Can be carried out in respect of multiple search terms, individuals, groups or organizations	
Require researcher to assess relevance in relation to material identified	
Can capture different forms of Internet data	
Results determined by algorithms of proprietary tools and platforms	
Can be adapted at any stage (with some limitation on tracking as noted above) by researcher	
Can be used to supplement the results of the other method	

We have mentioned Google Alerts as an example of a proprietary tool that can be used for tracking and this is the tool we have used most in our own research. But there are several other options (not all of which were available when we set up data collection for our Age at Work project). While we are not recommending any specific tool, it is useful to note that there are many options, including tools specific to particular **data sources**, so the reader will need to explore which might work best in their own project. We discuss this further in later chapters of the book. New tools are likely to be developed over time. Some are primarily designed for data analytics and media monitoring, for example, coverage of brands and organizations. Some tools are free, some require a degree of technical skill to use and some only cover specific types of web material. None of them are designed for academic research and the use of any of them, including Google Alerts, will determine what material is available to be collected as data as a result of the algorithms they run. The researcher is well advised to bear this in mind in relation to how they describe their data and the nature of the claims they make in their findings. All data are constructed in some way, but it is advisable for the researcher to be as transparent as possible in writing up their methodology.

We conclude our introduction to tracking and trawling with a note of caution about what they are not. Although the methods could be used to investigate how people use the Internet, they are not themselves concerned with this. As we noted above, they are different from netnography (and digital or online ethnography), which tend to be methods where the researcher is immersed in the specific location of study. In tracking and trawling the researcher is outside the location that they are studying, though they may come close to the location through their own digital activities (over time, our own blog posts occasionally appeared in the Google Alerts we had set up for data collection). But broadly there is a different relationship here between the researcher and the research topic than in an ethnographic context.

OUR APPROACH TO THIS BOOK

This book is primarily aimed at those undertaking a Masters research project in the field of business and management. We assume that as Masters students these readers will have little or no experience of using digital methods of data collection. However, in discussion with peers and colleagues, we learnt that the material was likely to be of use to more experienced researchers who are either interested in learning more about these digital methods or are supervising those who are doing so. With that in mind, we have included examples of published work in Chapter 5 that introduce additional aspects of digital methods that are appropriate for further or advanced research in this area.

In terms of the structure of the book, the rest of the chapters take a broadly chronological approach to the steps required across the duration of a research project. Chapter 2 introduces readers to key aspects of the philosophy of research and explains how these impact on collecting qualitative digital data via tracking and trawling in a business and management research project. Chapter 3 discusses the components of the tracking and trawling methods, identifying the generic stages involved in such research with advice regarding issues to consider and address at each stage. Chapter 4 considers the way in which the different components may be organized to use the method, focusing on the practical aspects of each of the stages. Chapters 2, 3 and 4 are illustrated with worked examples of possible Masters projects. Chapter 5 provides more detailed illustrations of how collecting qualitative digital data has been used in published studies in business and management research. Chapter 6 concludes by reflecting on the strengths and weaknesses of that method, including assessing quality in digital qualitative research by paradigm-appropriate criteria. The chapter also contains some tips on preparing for data analysis.

Throughout the book we have used the term 'collect' and 'collecting', however, it is commonly acknowledged with **qualitative research** that data are **constructed** and **curated** through the research process. While there are different stances taken, as we explore in Chapter 2, many agree that data do not exist separately from and prior to the research project. Rather, data 'become' through the research process; as indeed does the researcher. We develop what this means for the researcher undertaking tracking and trawling throughout the book, particularly in Chapters 3 and 4.

Given the structure and relatively modest length of the book it makes most sense for it to be read from start to finish and then dipped into again as necessary and useful to support specific stages in the Masters research project. We are enthusiastic about the possibilities of digital methods for examining issues in business and management and use examples from our own research to illustrate many of the points discussed in the book. For us, the following quote by Annette Markham summarizes the considerable scope and impact of the Internet for those conducting qualitative research:

> In terms of qualitative inquiry, the Internet does not simply provide new tools or venues for conducting social research, it challenges taken-for-granted frameworks for how identities, relationships, cultures, and social structures are constructed. Likewise, it challenges how we understand and conduct qualitative inquiry in an epoch of media convergence, mediated identities, redefinitions of social boundaries, and the transcendence of geographical boundaries. (Markham, 2010: 112)

We hope this book provides a helpful and accessible guide to those wishing to take advantage of these opportunities of using digital methods in the field of qualitative business and management research. No research is ever perfect but our aim here is to ensure that planning and being prepared ensures that when issues and challenges arise, as they surely will, the researcher is well placed to address them.

2

UNDERSTANDING TRACKING AND TRAWLING

INTRODUCTION

The aim of this chapter is to examine how tracking and trawling methods can be used in different ways, depending on the broader philosophical orientation of the research project. This is an important consideration because to answer the research questions posed, the way in which a method is implemented needs to be aligned to the philosophical assumptions made by the researcher.

For more traditional methods, there are extensive debates regarding relationships with particular philosophical assumptions. Such discussions of methodological 'fit' are also supported by published examples of empirical studies that demonstrate how a particular philosophical stance translates into research practice. However, since tracking and trawling are relatively new approaches, and the broader field of online research is rapidly developing, such debates are nascent and fewer examples are available. In this chapter, we therefore provide a recap of the different approaches that may guide a research undertaking and explore the ways tracking and trawling can be applied. As we examine, this requires the researcher to reflect on the three questions of what, where and who as outlined in the introduction.

The following topics are explored in this chapter:

- philosophical assumptions
- different approaches to tracking and trawling
- qualitative post-positivism
- interpretivist studies
- critical approaches.

PHILOSOPHICAL ASSUMPTIONS

The overviews of tracking and trawling offered in this book are not tightly bound to particular research orientations or philosophies. However, most researchers approach a project with either an implicit or explicit theoretical framework that shapes the way in which the project unfolds. Therefore, how tracking and trawling will be actually implemented in practice will be driven by the researcher's own philosophical assumptions. Such assumptions are neither inherently right nor wrong, simply different.

Most commonly, such assumptions are reviewed according to the researcher's assumptions about:

1. The nature of reality; or **ontological assumptions**.
2. The way in which we can understand and generate knowledge; or **epistemological assumptions**.

In considering ontology, Duberley et al. (2012: 17) highlight that 'Ontological questions concern whether or not the phenomenon that we are interested in actually exists independently of our knowing and perceiving it'. Relatedly, epistemology concerns the philosophy of knowledge and the ways in which knowledge claims can be asserted and defended, debates which can be traced back at least as far as Plato and Aristotle (Morton, 1977). Unsurprisingly such issues are the subject of extensive, some might say exhausting, debate within academic literature. Given the focus of this book on online methods it is pertinent to note that notions of reality and knowledge online add a further twist to such debates. These are no longer simply academic concerns (Lazer et al., 2018), but issues such as **'fake news'** and **deepfake online videos** are topics of public debate (Bellemare, 2019; Chivers, 2019).

Returning to research philosophy, there are many classifications of the ways in which different assumptions combine that give rise to labels for research orientations. Within the modest confines of this book we do not offer a detailed review of such classifications but outline areas of significant differences. Duberley et al. (2012) explain that, combining ontology and epistemology, the philosophical assumptions underpinning research are often presented as a difference between **realist** and **relativist** perspectives. Realist perspectives are based on assumptions that presume the objects of research are awaiting our discovery (ontology) via the application of appropriately objective and scientific methods (epistemology). This contrasts with a relativist perspective that challenges the notion of a 'concrete' reality (ontology), rather assuming reality comes into being via various and complex processes of construction (epistemology). Essentially then Duberley et al. suggest that 'if we reject the possibility of neutral observation, we have to admit to dealing with a socially constructed reality' (2012: 17).

A common criticism of debates about how a researcher might select their positioning and subsequent approach is that they are decontextualized. This runs the risk of presenting a somewhat idealized picture of a researcher who is completely in control of the direction of the research project. In other words, we risk assuming a 'pure' research project. However, researchers and research projects are influenced by many different stakeholders and many might be better described as 'applied'. In the case of applied research, it is still useful to unpack the philosophical assumptions held by different stakeholders to ensure that the research design meets expectations. We return to this in Chapter 4. Having outlined the different basis for philosophical assumptions, we now explore how these will impact the research design in the follow section.

DIFFERENT APPROACHES TO TRACKING AND TRAWLING

In this section, we explore how the design of a qualitative tracking or trawling study might be influenced by the philosophical assumptions driving the research project. To unpack these issues, we use the general differences between realist and relativist positioning explored in the previous section but, given our focus on qualitative research, we are going to unpack this slightly further based on the way in which experience is understood. This gives us three rather than two categories for consideration:

1. **Qualitative post-positivism**: This perspective aligns to the realist position outlined previously: that real phenomena have to be specified and discovered via objective and scientific methods. While this is most commonly associated with quantitative perspectives, it can similarly underpin a qualitative study. In such cases, there is usually a softening of the notion of a unifying common reality, since different framings of experience are recognized. However, qualitative approaches usually emphasize an objective methodological stance and many approaches can therefore be included here. Eriksson and Kovalainen (2015) include **critical realism**, **symbolic interactionism** and **grounded theory** under this heading.

2. **Interpretivist**: This covers a broad range of research that usually includes those falling under the closely related labels of **hermeneutics** (Wernet, 2014) and **phenomenology** (Eberle, 2014). While we have grouped these perspectives together in this book, it is advised that researchers further explore the specific commitments entailed in the different 'flavours' of an interpretivist undertaking. Research from this perspective is concerned with **meaning making** and so the object of research is individual or collective experience of a particular aspect of reality.

3. **Critical approaches**: It is again important to recognize the broad nature of this label that we are using here in a relatively simplistic way (Eriksson and Kovalainen, 2015). This covers research that questions the nature of reality and the ways in which we come to understand it, usually invoking a political aspect to unpick how our experiences are shaped. The key contrast with the research that we position under an interpretivist label is the **decentring of individual meaning** in favour of attending to **deconstructing meaning** itself.

In the sections that follow, each of these is expanded and examples of tracking and trawling studies are provided.

QUALITATIVE POST-POSTIVISM

As outlined above, research proceeding under this broad heading starts from the assumption of a concrete reality that can be accessed by objective research methods. At first glance online research appears to be a particularly attractive opportunity for researchers who start from this perspective. First, 'online' is now a universally acknowledged context for human activity (Fielding et al., 2008). Whatever the technological science that facilitates our digital experiences, we have become accustomed to 'going' online and 'posting' on the web as though it were a physical place. In this sense, it has become accepted as real; a reality that warrants investigation (Kiesler, 2014). Second, for many the web is an easily accessed 'place', and we often make assumptions about the status of what is displayed on our **devices**. For example, we tend to assume that we can all access the same information via various interfaces and portals. This leads to an everyday understanding of the status of online information as uniformly shared. From this perspective of research, 'objects' can be easily defined. Third, the separation between our 'offline' existence and our 'online' experiences seem to offer a means of creating an objective distance for the researcher. This is a common feature of many methods. For instance, the construction of a questionnaire as a research tool creates a distance between the researcher and participants who may never directly come into contact. Online research also provides the potential for such separation, which is seen as critical for research objectivity. This is particularly the case when the researcher can separate their research activity from personal experiences by setting up specific accounts or profiles that are used solely for research.

As we will see further below, these positions are considered problematic by those who adopt an interpretivist or critical stance. However, even within research communities that align with a post-positivist positioning there are concerns that the apparent ease of access to online data can lead to poorly designed studies (Fielding et al., 2008). It is therefore important, as with any other mode of research, for the design process to clearly define the parameters of the research question under consideration and that the variables of research are well understood. In the context of online research, the variables are more extensive. Specifically, **technological and platform variables** will need further consideration during the design stage. This will include issues such as devices used, **mode of access**, **origin of access** (including the **Internet Protocol (IP) address** that drives characteristics such as language displayed), **online identity** or profile used for research, means of access and platform or target of research. These factors may all need to be recorded as metadata later in the project. While these issues need to be considered across all research projects, because of the commitment to objectivity made within a post-positive stance, the basis for this must be established at the outset.

Returning to our questions of what, who and where for online research, we explore these in further detail in Table 2.1.

Table 2.1 Applying qualitative post-positive assumptions

	Applying qualitative post-positive assumptions	Implications for data collection
What?	The concept or variables under investigation can be clearly identified in advance of the study from previous studies (including those not using web-based data).	The key terms that will drive data collection are already established. There will be some form of assessment of sources identified to ensure they fit the scope of the study.
Who?	The actors or sources who might participate in the study can be clearly identified in advance. The researcher does not feature within the study but is separate from it.	A target will be defined for data collection. The nature of the target will differ for tracking and trawling studies, but in both cases suitable criteria can be defined by the researcher. Flexibility to extend the range of targets may be defined subject to specific criteria. Criteria for objectivity may be factored into research design such as the use of different technical tools and interfaces.
Where?	The specific locations online for data collection and the means for accessing these are known.	The field of study will be defined prior to data collection. Technological and platform variables are identified. Technical tools for targeting the object of study will need to be tested to ensure access fits pre-defined criteria.

Having outlined the overall framework for tracking and trawling from a post-positivist stance, below (in Boxes 2.1 and 2.2) we offer two illustrative examples of studies that adopt such an approach.

Box 2.1   A qualitative post-positivist tracking study

Mia is a Masters student who is studying part-time while working in the HR department of a large insurance company. Working with her manager, she is designing a study exploring how other UK financial institutions are using social media to communicate

(Continued)

their commitment to diversity. She is using the FTSE100 to define which financial institutions she should include in her study, and the UK Equality Act for a definitive list of different aspects of diversity she should consider. Working with her manager, Mia has also come up with a classification of different communication types based on an understanding of social media platform use. She is particularly keen to distinguish between the way in which firms might use social media to show support through sharing others' communications as opposed to initiating communication by holding events or making announcements.

Mia has been advised by her supervisor that she should search for other similar studies so that she can re-use an existing communications and platform classification as this will make her study more robust. At the moment, Mia is planning to use her own social media accounts to follow the list of companies she has identified via Twitter and **Instagram.** She hasn't yet completed her ethics form but is hoping to download all the data onto her laptop and is thinking of using a form of qualitative **content analysis.** Since her organization is paying for her studies, Mia has been asked to identify the key characteristics of effective communication and draw up a set of guidelines as a result of her analysis.

Box 2.2   A qualitative post-positivist trawling study

Jakob is undertaking a Masters by research into the way in which paternity leave is presented within the broader context of public debates about gender. Jakob does not have direct access to an organization or other group to explore this topic. Working with his supervisor, he has devised a study to sample specific news websites for articles published since April 2015 (the date of regulatory change). Jakob is targeting online newspapers that are known in the UK as 'broadsheets', since he believes these have a better reputation for reporting quality and are seen to be more reliable sources of news stories. He plans to download copies of all the sources he identifies and will classify these according to a typology he is developing in advance. This typology will group news stories according to whether they are positive, neutral or negative about paternity leave and then Jakob will randomly select a sub-set for more detailed case analysis of each theme. Jakob is going to meet with his supervisor to review the outcomes of his data collection before he proceeds with analysis.

These examples offer insight into the framing of a research project from this perspective; however, there are further issues to be explored during the detailed research design as will be explored in the subsequent chapters of this book.

INTERPRETIVIST STUDIES

As highlighted above, for the sake of simplicity in our account we are treating research under this broad label as having comparable aims and encountering similar issues when undertaking tracking and trawling. Interpretivist research seeks to understand experience and the way in which individuals or groups make sense of such experience. From this perspective, online research is attractive as the experiential nature of the web may potentially be much easier to access than offline contexts. Initially researchers sought specific 'places' on the web to research from this perspective, particularly sites where certain topics were discussed or where groups with certain characteristics met. Much of this research has been pursued via interactive methodologies such as online ethnography (Hine, 2008) or netnography (Kozinets, 2010).

However, tracking and trawling are attractive for interpretivist studies since they offer a means of accessing the area of research interest without the more complex and time-consuming participant-observation approaches. Indeed, we would suggest that a tracking or trawling type study might be a useful preliminary step for a more in-depth ethnographic-inspired approach since it might offer initial insights that can guide the design of such a study. An example of a study that combines a more in-depth case approach with online research (Orlikowski and Scott, 2014) is reviewed in Chapter 5, although the extensive nature of this and similar studies means they go beyond the parameters of many Masters research projects.

The key challenges for an interpretivist tracking and/or trawling study is the approach taken to understanding the way in which meaning making is experienced online. Within the approaches of tracking and trawling we have outlined in this book, we deliberately exclude direct contact between the researcher and 'live' participants (whether contacted online or in person). However, in Chapter 3 we include an example of a Masters research project where tracking and trawling could be combined with interviews and in Chapter 5 we provide examples of how tracking and trawling can be used in conjunction with other methods that involve participants. Our focus is the collection of material that has or is being made available online for purposes other than the specific research study being undertaken. This introduces a related concern of many qualitative researchers: **authenticity on the web** (Thurlow, 2018). Concerns with authenticity are premised on the idea that pretty much anyone can post anything online. Many groups, sites and forums are open and, as already discussed, 'faking it' is now a well-established genre online. Given interpretivists are interested in meaning making, the question of authenticity is particularly relevant. What if the materials collected are in some way false or even malicious? Of course, this can never entirely be ruled out, but a careful research design can incorporate steps to mitigate against this. These might include targeting specific sources or sites, cross-checking key topics and following established research protocols from previous empirical studies. Tracking provides a further facility in this regard as it offers a means of following an issue over time, allowing the researcher to develop a better understanding of the issue under consideration. It is, however, important to consider that, similar to how we trust the spoken words exchanged within an interview as providing access to individual meaning, we may need to trust the online posts collected via tracking and trawling.

A related issue here concerns the way in which institutions might be represented online and the variability between voices across different roles and platforms. For example, an organizational Twitter account might be taken as the 'voice' of an organization. However, from an interpretivist perspective, the role of different individuals, and the sense that this might not be representative of a true voice, will be more problematic for research purposes.

In a significant shift from a post-positivist position, with an interpretivist stance comes recognition of the researcher's role in all aspects of the research process, usually through a commitment to reflexivity. Reflexivity is held as a crucial aspect of research practice through which we might (briefly but repeatedly) shift our focus from the phenomena under investigation to question our role(s) as researchers in the production of knowledge; it is also a means of enabling learning about the research process and thereby understanding how it might be improved (Alvesson and Skoldberg, 2000; Yanow and Tsoukas, 2009). Reflexivity is said to offer the potential, as Rhodes (2009: 656) suggests, 'for research to recognize itself as creative practice'.

There are two significant issues to consider from this commitment to reflexivity. First, the researcher should consider their own experiences of and engagement with online contexts both prior to and throughout the research process. Second, that it is possible to use online environments (such as a blog) to facilitate the research process in ways that may have the effect of fully embedding the researcher's own ideas and thoughts into the data collection process.

Returning to our questions of what, who and where for online research, we explore these in further detail in Table 2.2 in relation to interpretivist assumptions.

Table 2.2   Applying interpretivist assumptions

	Applying interpretivist assumptions	Implications for data collection
What?	The scope of the study will be broadly defined and an area of interest mapped out.	A range of terms will drive data collection.
		Boundaries about what is included/excluded are likely to emerge during a pilot or in the early stages of the study.

	Applying interpretivist assumptions	Implications for data collection
Who?	An initial group, set of voices or range of individuals will have been identified as a starting point. There is likely to have been a preliminary investigation of these online to identify the characteristics.	An appropriate scale of study to achieve necessary depth will be required. Given this, the range of voices under consideration is likely to be relatively small. Issues may relate to institutional voices online where a variety of different people may be communicating at different times or across different channels.
Where?	There will be interest in the types of online environment used and how these might differ.	Some types of sites might be intuitively more attractive given the way in which they are typically used. For instance, blogs have typically been viewed as a type of online diary that are seen to capture lived experience.

Having outlined the overall framework for tracking and trawling from an interpretivist stance, below (in Boxes 2.3 and 2.4) we offer two illustrative examples of studies that adopt such an approach.

Box 2.3   An interpretivist tracking study

Charlie is studying for a Masters in marketing. She is keen to understand how those working in marketing perceive the usefulness of professional knowledge in 'real life' and how they make sense of continuing professional development (CPD). She has identified that many marketing professionals use a closely related set of Twitter hashtags to tweet about their professional development activities and experiences. Indeed, one of the hashtags seems to be widely used across Europe and the USA. Discussing this with her dissertation supervisor, Charlie plans to track these hashtags for a period of eight weeks and collect relevant tweets. While some researchers (Wasim, 2019) advise selecting a random sample for detailed **thematic analysis**, Charlie plans to first group the tweets by area of marketing knowledge using a high-level thematic analysis. From this initial thematic review, she then plans to select three knowledge themes for further detailed thematic analysis. She has discussed with her supervisor that she may select exemplar tweets for more detailed

(Continued)

analysis within her dissertation as she has seen this approach adopted in other stud-ies of digital data (Breitbarth et al., 2010). She also plans to follow links highlighted in these tweets to collect data about events taking place during this timeframe and hopes to incorporate an analysis of these websites to understand how meaningful CPD is presented to the profession. Her supervisor has advised her to be careful to manage the scale of the research project but agrees that exploring different avenues during data collection is a useful approach. They agree to meet to review the data she has collected and refine her research questions and analytic approach.

Box 2.4   An interpretivist trawling study

Henny is keen to conduct a research project as part of their MBA. They have a particular interest in sustainability. Henny has been reading about how small com-panies in the automotive sector position themselves in the 'green' market place. They are particularly keen to understand how being 'green' makes sense to these smaller companies within the broader context of the automotive sector. Henny has discussed a data collection strategy with their MBA project supervisor. From a recent sector report, they have identified a number of key terms that they can use in a digital search strategy. From an initial review, Henny already knows that this report received a lot of coverage across a range of online news from the popular press and in some more specialist news outlets that cover the sector. However, rather than just 'track' media mentions of this report going forward, Henny has decided to use a 'trawling' approach and use the search terms they have identi-fied in a broader search of online news. Their MBA project supervisor agrees that this is a useful approach for data collection but has advised Henny that they will need to be careful to draw boundaries around this data collection to avoid being overwhelmed.

Charlie and Henny's ideas for their research projects highlight some of the impor-tant considerations for undertaking a research project from this perspective in relation to choice of topic and approach to data identification. However, as we explore in subsequent chapters, both of these projects require more detailed design and plan-ning before data collection begins.

CRITICAL APPROACHES

As above, we recognize that 'critical approaches' is a broad category encompassing many different types of research, and indeed there has been much debate about the usefulness of this as an umbrella term given the breadth of positions adopted (Eriksson and Kovalainen, 2015). However, it is noteworthy that the label '**critical management studies**' has become well established. In general, these approaches often share an interest in experience with the interpretivist approach; however, such experience tends to be explored differently by taking a relativist stance and subjective approach. The question of **personal meaning** is therefore **problematized**. Research focuses instead on the different forces and influences that shape the presentation (textual, visual, material) of different realities rather than seeking to access personal meaning making. More specifically there is a focus on the way in which management (in either broad terms or in relation to a particular aspect) is socially and culturally situated. Critical approaches often attend to difficult or negative aspects of contemporary organizational life with the aim of enabling change.

From this perspective, pursuing research online offers some advantages. First, there is tremendous scope to explore the variety of presentations of a topic of interest and an opportunity to examine accounts for traces of dominant voices, representations and interests. The ability to follow different sources and trace connections may also provide a means of investigating the potential impact of different narratives. Second, ways in which critical research seeks to decentre the individual and focus on the account provided can seem more straightforward when faced with information gathered online. This is because the individual may already be hidden or obscured by technological means. Of course, this varies enormously and, conversely, within visual and multimedia sources individuals may be hyper-present depending on the media and platform combinations at play. This **dilemma of representation** is an aspect to which we particularly attend in our own research (Whiting and Pritchard, 2019). Third, because of the use of online media by many different institutional, organizational and other groups to engage in debate, some topics that might be seen as sensitive issues to research in person may be more accessible online. Of course, this does not make these topics themselves any less sensitive and appropriate. Ethical consideration regarding both the participants and the researcher are important here.

Furthermore, a critical research agenda is often seen as an opportunity for more creative research approaches and may seek to incorporate an emancipatory element. In both regards, online research might offer considerable potential, though of course neither are guaranteed. Critical research approaches also require a sceptical positioning. This relates to both the topic of research but also the means through which knowledge about the topic is generated. In this case then it is important to consider how a sceptical view of the Internet, social media and other forms of technological mediation might impact the research. All these aspects require a reflexive orientation towards research in which the researcher is required to open themselves and their assumptions to critical inquiry (Table 2.3 below).

Table 2.3 Applying critical assumptions

	Applying critical assumptions	Implications for data collection
What?	The topics of inquiry will be identified in advance but will be closely intertwined with questions of who and where. The topic is not assumed to be value free but associated with a particular set of interests.	Given the centrality of language to many critical studies the use of search terms and key words needs careful consideration.
		There may be a close association between certain terms and interests; this may enable a depth but restrict the breadth of data collection.
Who?	As outlined above, the who is likely to be integral to the study, as identification of interests will be central to the design of the research.	In a smaller scale project it will be key to identify the principal voices to be considered within the study.
		However, it is important to recognize that unexpected voices and participants can emerge and an approach to dealing with these is essential.
Where?	A critical approach will extend to questioning the neutrality of the online environment and will consider the active engagement of various media with the study.	The nature of platforms and the technological mediation of knowledge will likely need consideration within the research design.

Having outlined the overall framework for tracking and trawling from a critical stance, below we offer two illustrative examples (in Boxes 2.5 and 2.6) of studies that adopt such an approach.

Box 2.5   A critical tracking study

Alwyn is studying for a Masters by research after working in the public sector for over ten years. He is interested in understanding how being innovative, creative and having ideas about 'intrapreneurship' are increasingly promoted as essential attributes across a range of careers in public services. He recognizes his own discomfort with this idea will shape his study and has discussed this in his supervision meetings. Alwyn has decided to focus on the ways in which professional development training courses are targeting middle managers in the public sector with opportunities to develop these skills and attributes. His plan is to use various social media platforms to identify specific courses that are being promoted and follow links to collect online course details. At this stage he anticipates using discourse analysis to review course descriptions and unpack how the innovative and creative public sector worker is being constructed.

Box 2.6   A critical trawling study

Gwen is undertaking a Masters research project and is interested in exploring how adventure fundraising opportunities are promoted in the third sector. They are particularly interested in exploring how subject positions such as the donor/sponsor, active participant and the intended recipients of charitable donations are constructed. After discussion with their supervisor, they plan to pilot a number of search terms to test and also undertake a pilot search of Instagram and Twitter. Their supervisor has suggested that the volume of data may be very high, and Gwen may need to narrow their search to trawl for a particular type of activity and/or charity type. Gwen agrees that they will review the search parameters during the pilot as they are keen to ensure they can conduct an in-depth analysis of the potential subject positions identified.

As we can see, the critical orientation is explicit in the conception of these projects as both seek to unpack and unpick particular positionings. In subsequent chapters, we explore key issues that these students would need to address before data collection begins.

CHAPTER SUMMARY

In this chapter we have:

- explored how a researcher's philosophical orientation shapes a research project
- considered different orientations towards tracking and trawling
- provided a review of the way in which three broad research orientations (post-positivist, interpretivist and critical approaches) can shape tracking and trawling
- reviewed each of these orientations in more detail, setting out the considerations for undertaking both tracking and trawling studies.

When considering a Masters research project, it is advisable to consult widely regarding the philosophical issues and consider personal perceptions of the topic being explored. In tracking and trawling studies, as highlighted earlier, it is also critical to take account of personal perceptions of online spaces, platforms and actors. References within this chapter and elsewhere in the book contain many detailed **resources** to assist in this task.

3

BASIC COMPONENTS OF TRACKING AND TRAWLING METHODOLOGY

INTRODUCTION

The aim of this chapter is to provide the detail of what is required when collecting, and preparing to collect, qualitative digital data using the tracking and trawling method. It identifies and explains the generic stages involved in this methodology, linking these where appropriate to the underlying research approach, including the ethical considerations of qualitative Internet data. We illustrate these stages with examples from our own research and examples from fictional student projects. The chapter also provides advice regarding issues to consider and address at each of these stages, anticipating the option of moving between the tracking and trawling approaches and explaining how these are related.

The following generic stages of the methodology are reviewed in this chapter:

- designing research questions
- deciding on data type(s)
- designing data collection
- data selection and sampling strategy
- choosing data selection tools
- examining ethical issues
- designing data management
- choosing a data management method
- conducting a pilot study
- conducting the main study
- data management and preparing for analysis.

DESIGNING RESEARCH QUESTIONS

Designing the research questions for a project is very much interconnected with the underlying philosophical orientation that the researcher is adopting. As explored in the previous chapter, the decisions that the researcher makes in respect of their research about the nature of reality (ontological assumptions) and the way in which we understand and generate knowledge (epistemological assumptions) will determine how the research questions are designed and worded. In Table 3.1 we show the research questions that would underpin the examples of Masters research projects that we introduced in Chapter 2.

Table 3.1 Examples of research questions from worked examples of Masters projects

Type of study	Example	Research question
A qualitative post-positivist tracking study	Chapter 2: Box 2.1 (Mia)	How do UK financial institutions use social media to communicate their commitment to diversity?
A qualitative post-positivist trawling study	Chapter 2: Box 2.2 (Jakob)	To what extent is paternity leave presented as a positive development in media discussions about gender equality?
An interpretivist tracking study	Chapter 2: Box 2.3 (Charlie)	In what ways do marketing professionals perceive continuing professional development as useful?
An interpretivist trawling study	Chapter 2: Box 2.4 (Henny)	In what ways can SMEs in the automotive sector position themselves on social media in relation to understandings of 'greenness'?
A critical tracking study	Chapter 2: Box 2.5 (Alwyn)	Who is the innovative and creative public sector worker?
A critical trawling study	Chapter 2: Box 2.6 (Gwen)	In what ways do social media campaigns about adventure fundraising create distinctive subject positions for those involved?

As can be seen in Table 3.1, interpretivist and critical studies are more likely to involve research questions that ask 'how' or 'in what ways'. Post-positivist studies are more likely to involve research questions that ask 'what'. Published academic papers on a proposed research topic will also provide the Masters researcher with a sense of how the underpinning ontological and epistemological assumptions of the research are linked to the research design, including the formulation of research questions.

Some papers will set out their research questions very clearly and explicitly. In other cases, it is necessary to read the abstract and methods section of a paper quite carefully to distil the research aim or question. Further examples of research questions from published studies are given in Chapter 5.

For a Masters research project, a good research question needs to be clearly worded, it needs to set out exactly what it is (concept, phenomenon or construct, etc.) that will be examined and may, for completeness, need to incorporate the research context in which the proposed study will take place. If the context is not part of how the research question is formulated, then it needs to be clearly explained in the introduction to the research project when this is written up. The aim is to ensure that the reader is clear as to what is being investigated and in what context. It is good practice to repeat this detail at various points in the project report such as the methodology, findings and discussion sections.

While the project is still ongoing, being clear about the research question will help the researcher stay focused, for example, in terms of deciding what is or is not relevant data. In common with research using other qualitative methods, however, it is quite likely that the original research question may develop a little over the course of the project, as the researcher reacts to the nature of the data collected. We include suggestions for keeping focus and handling the possible evolution of a research question in more detail in Chapter 4.

DECIDING ON DATA TYPE(S)

The scope of the research question will largely drive the type(s) of data to be collected. This should always be piloted. See below to assess the efficacy of the method of data collection and the ability of the data to address the research question. It may be that more than one method of data collection is required. We discussed in Chapter 1 how tracking and trawling represent opposite points on a spectrum of ways of collecting Internet data and that a project might involve a combination of the two. Depending on the research question, it might also involve combining Internet data with other **data types** (such as interviews) in what is usually referred to as a multi-method design (see Baxter and Marcella, 2017).

The Internet provides a vast range of possible types of qualitative data that can be textual or visual. Examples include tweets, websites, blogs, Instagram postings, articles from news media (which might include stock images or cartoons), **YouTube** videos and **Facebook** pages. In fact, multi-modality is such a key feature of web material that many Internet data sources will combine texts and images. This means the researcher will need to decide whether to examine textual data (Pritchard and Whiting, 2014), visual data (Davison, 2010) or both (Benschop and Meihuizen, 2002). For a Masters research project it may be easier to restrict data to one mode (either textual or visual) since whatever data are collected will need to be analysed; there are a range of analytic methods designed specifically for each mode of data, which could easily extend the scope of the project beyond the given timeframe and permitted word count.

Some potential data are material that have traditionally existed as published documents such as corporate annual reports and which are now routinely made available on an organization's websites. As Davison (2010) explains, annual reports are the main channel for reporting financial information for organizations, but their content has expanded over time to include material that is not required by the financial regulators (such as pictures) but which companies choose to add. Other types of potential data are in forms developed specifically for the web and which did not exist pre-Internet, such as websites, **discussion forums**, blogs and tweets. There are also data types that represent a traditional form such as news stories which have moved online. In doing so, this has opened up new data possibilities, for example, through the wider inclusion of stock photographs within online news stories and the introduction of below-the-line comments, which have largely replaced letters to the editor as a means for readers to respond to news items.

For examples of specific forms of textual Internet data, see Boland's (2016) analysis of job search websites in respect of job advertisements and advice targeted at the job seeker, Glozer et al.'s (2019) study of organizational legitimation through social media dialogue using the public corporate Facebook pages of two contrasting companies, and Ozdora-Aksak and Atakan-Duman's (2015) study of Turkish banks' use of Facebook and Twitter to understand the role of public relations in how organizational identity is constructed. Other examples of textual data include blogs and online news media stories. For examples of specific forms of visual Internet data, see Duff's (2011) critical photo analysis of images in corporate annual reports to examine the intersection of accounting, gender and race, and Rokka and Canniford's (2016) visual content analysis of consumer-made **selfies** featuring champagne brands on Instagram. Other types of visual data could include stock photographs, cartoons and YouTube videos (see also Chapter 5).

DESIGNING DATA COLLECTION

Once the researcher has decided on their research questions and identified their potential data types, then they are ready to design their data collection, which includes selecting their data sources. While the focus in this book is on the Internet data, the researcher may intend to combine Internet data with another method (such as interviews), in which case this needs to be factored into the design.

A helpful starting point is to think about the design of the data collection in terms of what, who and where, the framing we introduced in the earlier chapters. Briefly, *what* relates to the topic of interest and scope of the study; *who* relates to the organization(s), group(s) or individuals who are the focus of the topic; and *where* relates to the digital data sources on the Internet from which data will be collected. It will also be necessary to ensure that the design reflects the implications of the chosen approach (post-positivism, interpretivist or critical); see Chapter 2. Whichever approach is selected, the data collection may involve tracking or trawling or a combination of both as illustrated in the following examples.

Box 3.1 looks at data collection design using trawling in a study that adopts a qualitative post-positivist approach. It highlights the need for initial steps in the design process, before carrying out a more systematic pilot study to assess the robustness of the data collection method.

Box 3.1   Designing data collection for a qualitative post-positivist study using trawling

Ahmed is a full-time Masters student who wants to evaluate the scope of corporate social responsibility policies (the *what*) among large organizations in the UK (the *who*) as published on their corporate websites (the *where*). He has decided to use the FTSE100 to determine which organizations to include in his study. Since he is interested in a type of policy that is not subject to daily change, his focus is on the existing policies in place in these companies. This means that a trawling method of data collection will be appropriate as this is designed to collect materials that already exist. The key term that will drive data collection is 'corporate social responsibility' (CSR). However, Ahmed's supervisor suggested that he look at some sample websites of FTSE100 organizations to see what kinds of material are available in relation to corporate social responsibility and how these are described.

Ahmed has downloaded a list of FTSE100 companies from the web and identified potentially relevant parts of the websites of five of these companies by searching for their company name combined with the term 'corporate social responsibility' using a basic Internet search engine. In doing so, Ahmed has identified a range of different types of document, not just formal policies but statements, plans and sections of websites that refer to CSR but also use related terms (such as 'sustainability' and 'values'), perhaps reflecting the different sectors and practices of the organizations whose websites he had sampled.

This is interesting to him as he wants to focus on the scope of CSR policies. Cross-checking with the academic literature on CSR, Ahmed is able to develop a list of key terms to use in the next stage of his data collection.

In the next example (Box 3.2), we look at a study that uses both tracking and trawling to collect data in relation to research that adopts an interpretivist approach, and which combines web data with interviews. This highlights the flexibility of the tracking and trawling methodology as well as raising the issue of addressing ethical considerations as part of designing data collection.

Box 3.2   Designing data collection for an interpretivist study using tracking and trawling

Belinda is a part-time Masters student who is now working in the food retail sector. During her undergraduate degree she worked front of house in a local bistro and developed an interest in the careers of those working in the hospitality industry. She wants to use her graduate research project to investigate the occupational identity and culture (the *what*) of restaurant chefs and their brigades (the *who*). From her stint in the local restaurant and her current role, she knows that there is some anonymous material online written by those working in the industry and she also has some personal contacts working in restaurant kitchens. Her supervisor has suggested that she might combine interviews with web data as it is not clear how many people Belinda might be able to recruit to her study as the prospective interview participants work extremely long hours.

Focusing on material online, Belinda has located a number of blogs (the *where*) written by people currently working in kitchen brigades. She was aware of a few such blogs from her work in the sector but finds more through using an Internet search engine, using key words from blogs already identified. Most of these are anonymous as they provide an insider account (not always very flattering) of life working in some high-profile restaurants. This raises ethical concerns (and see the section on ethics below), which Belinda must address in the design of both her web and interview data collection, where key concerns are to protect the anonymity of participants and preserve the confidentiality of their data. For ethical purposes, the authors of the blogs are regarded as participants.

Following discussion with her supervisor, Belinda identifies a number of blogs that relate to life working in UK-based restaurants. She decides that she will use both the existing blog posts that are already available online (identified through trawling) and will track for additional material which is posted to the blogs over the next six months. This is made possible through the time-scale for her project on a part-time Masters degree.

In some cases, the blogs allow a viewer to sign up to receive an email notification when a new blog post appears online; others are linked to a Twitter account, which alerts followers in the same way. Belinda uses a combination of these methods to track new posts on her selected blogs. She sets up an email and Twitter account specifically for the research project into which these alerts are returned.

In the next example (Box 3.3), we look at designing data collection for a study that adopts a critical approach. This is a single case study of a corporate website that highlights the inherent multi-modality of the website by including both visual and textual data in the data collection design.

Box 3.3   Designing data collection for a study using a critical approach using tracking and trawling

Carla is a part-time Masters student who is also working in public relations. She is interested in the broad topic of management communication and wants to look at how corporate websites are used in disaster communication. Having read some critical management studies papers in this area, some of which use both visual and textual data, her choice of a corporate website reflects her conceptualization of this as an interactive and visual communication tool.

She has read some academic papers on the BP Deepwater Horizon environmental catastrophe and her idea is to find an example of another organization that went through a similarly challenging PR episode, preferably where there is a suggestion of organizational wrongdoing. This reflects her critical management approach; her focus will be on the storytelling power of the corporate website and examining how corporate power is enabled through its use (the *what*).

Carla also identifies all pages of the website that relate to the disaster, including any images. Since she wants to track any changes or additions to the website, she then sets up a series of alerts (using a proprietary website tracking tool) which will notify her of any changes that are made to it.

After using an Internet search engine to identify examples of possible corporate disasters, Carla discusses a shortlist of these with her project supervisor. They consider the suitability of each as a possible case study for Carla's project. Their discussion is based on a consideration of the relevant website, its degree of multi-modality and the extent of online corporate material relating to the disaster, including the frequency of website updates. They consider the possibility of including social media data about the disaster but decide on balance that this might extend the scope of the project beyond the bounds of what is achievable within the required timespan.

Once they have made their decision regarding a suitable organizational case study (the *who*), Carla refines the design of the data collection. As the disaster has only occurred fairly recently, she anticipates that there will be further material added to the organization's corporate website (the *where*) in the weeks to follow. She therefore uses a combination of trawling and tracking. She trawls to find the homepage of the corporate website, which can be seen as the starting point for the particular disaster story (Kassinis and Panayiotou, 2017) and which functions 'like a magazine's front page ... [offering] a strong, though not compulsory, interpretive frame for what is to follow' (Pablo and Hardy, 2009: 826).

These examples show some of the ways in which tracking and trawling can be used as methods of data collection, either singly or together, on their own or in combination with other methods such as interviews, to address research questions across a range of possible approaches.

The final part of the data collection design is choosing the sources of digital data for the project. In the above examples, we have identified the data sources that each student selects as best able to address their research question. The process involves initial web browsing using an Internet search engine to gather some broadly relevant material but then refining this to identify specific sources based on a consideration of issues including available time for the project, the nature and modalities of the source, and whether updates or changes to it are required.

DATA SELECTION AND SAMPLING STRATEGY

Once the researcher has decided on their data, in broad terms they have addressed the *what*, *who* and *where* questions as in the above examples, they will need to decide how to select from the total material that is potentially available as data. For example, Glozer and colleagues (2019) provide a justification for selecting public Facebook pages as the social media focus of a study on organizational legitimation. Selection here was made on the basis 'of the scale of Facebook (over 1.94 billion monthly active users; Facebook, 2017), high frequency of interactions with this 'social network' ... rich textural cues (e.g. 'likes', 'shares'), as well as the lack of restriction on word limits for posts' (Glozer et al., 2019: 630). We discuss data selection in more detail in Chapter 5.

As this example illustrates, one of the advantages of Internet data is that there are often plenty to choose from; the challenge in such instances is therefore to work out an appropriate sampling strategy. This is an important part of the overall study design as it provides a rationale for the data selection in a way that provides a degree of transparency for those who read an account of the research including those who may wish to replicate or extend it.

Boland (2016) provides an example of data selection and sampling strategy in respect of research looking at UK websites that provide advice to the unemployed job seeker. In Boland's study, websites 'were selected because of their high page-rank on Google searches; around six on average' (2016: 340). Reading the material on each website allowed the author to determine when they had reached '**saturation sample**'. In other words, they used the concept of data saturation, denoted as being when no new information was being generated by additional websites (the author observed that these were just repeating information already obtained). We discuss the concept of data saturation further in the section of Chapter 4, 'Getting ready for analysis'.

There is no agreed view, however, within the academic literature on when such empirical data saturation is achieved (Francis et al., 2010). The absence of a consensus is largely due to the lack of explicit guidelines in qualitative research about what constitutes a credible sample size (Saunders and Townsend, 2018). Further or alternative views are that appropriate sample size depends on the claims you want to make about your findings and whether the data are going to be combined with other types of data (such as in Box 3.2 above of Belinda's Masters research project, which will combine blogs with interview data). This is an issue where students are advised to take advice from their project supervisor and where ongoing review is required, for example, in terms of the quality of the data. It may be the case that some data sources turn out to be less useful in addressing the research question than had been anticipated; extending the sample size is one potential solution.

CHOOSING DATA SELECTION TOOLS

This is the point where the researcher can decide whether to use only tracking or trawling (as in the example of Ahmed, Box 3.1) or a mixture of both (as in the examples of Belinda, Box 3.2, and Carla, Box 3.3). If the researchers are using a tracking approach, then they will be designing their data collection in a way that will capture new material being posted on the Internet going forwards in time from when they start. In other words, the data they collect will not exist at the time they start; it will be posted onto the Internet in a future period. If the researcher is using a trawling approach, then they will be designing their data collection in a way that captures material already published on the Internet prior to the start of their data collection. In other words, the data they collect exists at the time they start; it has already been posted on the Internet.

Trawling uses specific key word searches (such as in proprietary Internet search engines) to locate potentially relevant material in one or more web sources. These sources might be blogs, news sites, Twitter, YouTube, discussion forums, and other platforms such as **Mumsnet** and **Reddit**. Typically, data selection via trawling will then involve some narrowing down of the material identified through key word searches via the application of selection criteria or sampling strategy as we discuss in further detail in Chapter 5 when we examine examples in published studies. Tracking uses one or more proprietary tools such as Google Alerts to follow a group or organization, a particular event or a concept due to its engagement with a specific topic that is relevant to the research project. Again, we look at examples of published studies that have used this approach in Chapter 5.

Particularly in the case of tracking, the researcher is likely to be generating traffic in the form of (links to) material, which will need to be directed to an email address before being assessed for relevance and potential inclusion as data for their project. We would generally recommend the creation of a web-based project-specific email account (as in the case of Belinda, Box 3.2). This will act as a central repository for the alerts and other web material that the data collection methods create. It also protects the researcher's own personal or institutional email addresses from any spam or associated security issues.

EXAMINING ETHICAL ISSUES

In the context of qualitative research generally, ethics are broadly defined as the moral principles or rules of behaviour that guide research from inception through to publication and the curation of data. The main concern is to minimize risk of actual or potential harm while ensuring the maximum benefit of the research. The consideration of ethical issues in relation to collecting Internet data is one that is attracting increasing attention, with the position less clear and less well developed in terms of best practice than in relation to more traditional data collection methods such as interviews or focus groups.

Our focus here is to flag where the researcher can get specialist guidance and what we see as the major ethical issues for consideration. In doing so, we recognize that the research project will be conducted in a particular context (usually a department in a business or management school at a university), which will have its own ethical guidelines and procedures in place. These should always be the researcher's starting point. There may also be particular professional guidelines that apply. For example, a UK-based student in the field of organizational psychology would need to follow the Code of Human Research Ethics published by the **British Psychological Society** (BPS) in their research.

In addition to general institutional guidance, there is also specialist material from different social science perspectives and professional bodies that examines the ethics of Internet research (or some aspect thereof, such as social media). Some organizations, including the BPS, have issued specific guidelines in relation to Internet research, which will be useful to consider. Table 3.2 lists key examples (UK and international) with a brief description.

Table 3.2 Specialist guidance on Internet research

Authors	Title	Description
British Psychological Society (BPS)	British Psychological Society (2017). *Ethics Guidelines for Internet-mediated Research*. Leicester: British Psychological Society.	The BPS is the representative body for psychology and psychologists in the UK. This specialist guidance on Internet-mediated research is supplemental and subordinate to the Society's *Code of Human Research Ethics* (British Psychological Society, 2014) and to its overarching *Code of Ethics and Conduct* (British Psychological Society, 2009).
Economic & Social Research Council (ESRC)	ESRC (2015). *ESRC Framework for Research Ethics*. Updated January 2015. Swindon: Economic & Social Research Council.	The ESRC is one of the major research funders for those working in business and management studies in the UK. Its general ethics framework includes a section on Internet-mediated research. It identifies this as an area where university ethics committees might need to consult independent experts for their guidance on research proposals.

Authors	Title	Description
Association of Internet Researchers (AoIR)	Markham, A., and Buchanan, E. (2012). *Ethical Decision-Making and Internet Research: Recommendations from the AOIR Ethics Committee (Version 2.0)*: Association of Internet Researchers.	The AoIR is an international academic association set up to advance the cross-disciplinary field of Internet studies. In common with the BPS and ESRC, it recommends a contextualized, continual approach to ethical appraisal for Internet research.
L. Townsend and C. Wallace (University of Aberdeen)	Townsend, L., and Wallace, C. (2016). *Social Media Research: A Guide to Ethics*. Aberdeen: University of Aberdeen.	This guide specifically looks at ethics in social media research, and was developed as a result of research and workshop activities carried out by researchers at the University of Aberdeen, on an ESRC-funded project. The guidelines were co-produced by participants described as some of the 'key thinkers' in this area and include a handy decision-tree and case study examples.

Distilling some general guidance in relation to ethics from these various guidelines, the researcher should bear in mind the following points. Ethics in relation to Internet research ('digital ethics') must still follow the basic principles that apply to all research, namely to ensure that the research can be justified (including that the proposed design will address the research question), to ensure that participants (and the researcher) are protected from harm, and to obtain the informed consent of all those who take part in the study. However, using qualitative Internet data raises further issues as research practice in this area is less well developed than for, say, collecting interview data. As we see it (Whiting and Pritchard, 2017), there are four interrelated areas of debate: What is public or private on the Internet? Are we dealing with human participants? Do we need to obtain informed consent and, if so, from whom? Should we anonymize or attribute our data? We consider these questions below, setting out the key issues to be considered in addressing the ethics of qualitative Internet research.

One of the key challenges when using qualitative Internet data is determining whether the research involves human participants and thus whether informed consent should be obtained and, if so, from whom. In our example in Box 3.2, the authors of the blogs that Belinda proposes to use in her study should be regarded as human participants. This would require her to seek their informed consent for her to use their blog posts as data as well as giving them the option to further participate in her research as interviewees, which would require their further informed consent. In contrast, the research designed by Ahmed and Carla (Boxes 3.1 and 3.3) using organizational websites would not be seen as involving human participants as these comprise corporate public-facing material; consent to use this as data would not need to be sought. Determining human participation involves deciding whether we can distinguish between what people do on the Internet (send emails, upload photos, create profiles, comment on online media stories, write blogs) and their physical human identity.

The three-part test advocated by Schultze and Mason (2012) is very useful here. It asks researchers to consider the degree of entanglement (between the user's virtual manifestation on their blog, Facebook profile, tweets, etc. and their sense of self), the degree of interaction/intervention in the study (the extent to which the researcher becomes actively involved with the online material and the people who produce it) and the user's expectation of privacy. The higher the assessment of these three aspects, the more likely it is that human participation is involved and in which case, informed consent should be sought.

Critically, however, we would argue that seeking and obtaining ethics approval for both studies in the above examples is necessary as it is only by working through the nature of the proposed data and methods of collection that a student (and ethics committee) can assess the answers to the four questions we posed above. In terms of assessing what is private or public, early studies using qualitative Internet data rarely mentioned a consideration of ethics because web material was seen as secondary or archival data (Stablein, 2006). Organizational websites have been explicitly regarded as **public documents** available to analyse as if in printed form (for example, Coupland, 2005). Other studies applying **discursive** or **linguistic techniques** to analyse web-based data make little mention of the status of organizational websites (Billig, 2001; Coupland and Brown, 2004; Pablo and Hardy, 2009; Perren and Jennings, 2005; Sillince and Brown, 2009; Singh and Point, 2006), though the ethical status of 'public' web data is now a critical methodological debate. The key issue is that the Internet is not a single unitary location; it includes spaces, such as an online forum where people share information around a particular experience, where those using them would expect the information they share to be kept private (even if this material is publicly accessible). They certainly would not expect researchers to harvest this information uninvited and without seeking their consent or the consent of the forum site owner on their behalf.

We recognize that project supervisors and others involved in considering applications from students for ethical approval of their projects may be less familiar with digital ethics than the ethical principles of more traditional forms of data collection. It is sensible therefore for students to allow plenty of time for their ethics application as this may take longer to consider and approve. Since further work on this topic is being published all the time, for example, research papers that use Internet data and address digital ethics, we would also advise being familiar and keeping up to date with the latest practice in this area. Many publications do not include detailed consideration of ethical issues but where a study does mention particular challenges and how these were addressed this can be very useful. For instance, cloaking is a technique that involves changing data extracts by subtly paraphrasing them in such a way as to prevent readers from identifying the original site if they were to place text in a search engine. This has been seen as problematic in relation to textual analysis (Whiting and Pritchard, 2017) but Glozer and colleagues (2019) describe their use of cloaking in relation to the publication but critically not the analysis of their Facebook data; this can therefore be seen as an example of accepted practice in what is still a developing field.

DESIGNING DATA MANAGEMENT

One area that might be overlooked is designing the management of the data the researcher intends to collect. As we have discussed above, with qualitative Internet data, there could be numerous data types including both textual and visual data, which present a greater challenge than just, say, interview recordings and transcripts. The key is to anticipate this and plan how the data will be stored and managed. A number of considerations apply: keeping the data in a stable format (particularly given the inherently temporary and interactive nature of web material); maintaining data security; ensuring compliance with applicable legislative, regulatory and ethical requirements; enabling data search, retrieval and analysis; and considering subsequent publication (whether this is as a Masters research dissertation or as a conference paper, book chapter or journal article). We recommend checking what data management systems are available within the researcher's own institution; some universities or individual departments may have site licences for particular **computer assisted qualitative data analysis software** (CAQDAS). Although these are marketed as helping with analysis, they can also offer a mechanism for data management and organization as they generally involve the storage of raw data.

CHOOSING A DATA MANAGEMENT METHOD

We have been conducting research using Internet data for over ten years and during that time the options available for data management have evolved and increased; we expect that trend to continue so it is worth checking for new software solutions beyond those we mention here. **Achievability** (n.d.), a service provider for higher education in the area of Survey Data Analytics, has provided a list of CAQDAS available (as at July 2019), including **ATLAS.ti**, **AQUAD**, **Dedoose**, **MAXQDA**, **HyperRESEARCH**, **NVivo**, **QDA Miner**, **Tams Anayzler** and **Transana**. We should reiterate that we are not recommending any particular package. These vary in terms of the data formats that they support and some are more geared towards qualitative Internet data than others. Choice is therefore likely to be determined by the timescale, the scope and needs of the project, the types of web data to be used and any budget. Our non-exhaustive list includes one package that is free and open source (AQUAD) while the others are proprietary software. The latter are worth considering if readily available at the researcher's institution but can be expensive if researchers need to purchase them individually for themselves (we suggest checking to see if any free trials and/or reduced price student licences are available). Most CAQDAS packages are supported by online tutorials (in addition to training that universities may offer).

Some Internet data types require more bespoke storage and management solutions than others. For example, there are proprietary options for tracking changes made to websites over time, which allow for creating stable records of both the original and changed versions. This is useful for a research project where stability of data is usually critical. However, if the data being trawled is primarily text-based material available to be downloaded as Word documents or PDFs (say, annual reports) then there is less need for sophisticated software to achieve the same outcome. Data management might only require a secure password protected computer on which to store the materials using standard office software. Likewise, if data comprise material from corporate web pages, such as Ahmed's data (Box 3.1), the researcher has the option to cut and paste from the webpage into a Word document, to create a PDF of the page or to save the webpage for offline viewing. These methods create a permanent record of the webpage that captures the material as at the date of capture. Web data are often inherently multi-modal and these methods could also cope with data that included a limited number of visual images such as photos, charts, drawings or cartoons that might be part (but not the main focus) of the data. Obviously, the researcher would need to decide first whether such images would form part of their dataset and if so, how to collect, manage and later analyse them.

Other more uniquely web data types, such as tweets, Instagram posts and other social media forms, are more challenging to download into Word documents (and we have tried!). The advantage is that some CAQDAS packages have been developed to handle an increasing range of qualitative Internet data, which in some cases can be imported directly into the software. For example, at the time of writing (July 2020), the latest Windows edition of NVivo allows the direct importing of web data from Facebook, Twitter and YouTube. Other software may focus on specific forms of data. For example, Transana is specialist software for video and audio data though the Professional version (again, as at July 2020) also allows import and analysis of still images and text, including survey data. Researchers will need to decide what software (if any) is right for their project against a background of what is available, what they can afford and what is required in terms of data management and analysis. And whatever form of data management is established, the researcher will also need to maintain good practice in relation to broader IT routines such as ensuring regular back-ups of their work.

CONDUCTING A PILOT STUDY

One of the most common misunderstandings in relation to qualitative Internet data is that they are 'just there' and do not require any handling before the researcher can analyse them. This is emphatically not the case. Hence, running a pilot study of the data collection and management is a very sound idea. The scale of the pilot study needs to be proportional to the size of the main study and long enough to be able to see likely trends. To give an indication, we would suggest that if the researcher is planning to collect data over three months, then it would be sensible to run a pilot version for at least a week. Once the researcher has developed a research design this will require some experimentation to finalize the appropriate tool set (Pritchard and Whiting, 2012a). A key aim of the pilot therefore is to ensure that the proposed data collection tools actually generate the data required to address the research question. This involves not only assessing the proprietary tools themselves but how the researcher will use them, such as decisions over the scope of the settings that need to be decided (for example, choices over the language and the region(s) from which data will be collected, frequency of alerts and the specific search terms that will be used). To the extent that the data collected during the pilot study addresses the research question, this data can be incorporated into the main study data. If, however, the material generated in the pilot does not do so then it should be discarded as data. The other possibility is that some relevant data are generated but need to be substantially supplemented with additional data collection tools; in this case, the relevant material can be included as part of the main study data but it would be good practice to note the additional dates on which this material was collected.

By way of illustration, in our project on age at work, which examined web data collected over a six-month period, we initially piloted various search terms to use in Google Alerts and other proprietary tools over a period of four weeks. The search terms were developed partly from our literature search, which enabled us to focus on terms related to likely key topics in our subject area and partly from our own review of potentially relevant web material as we developed the overall design of the data collection. We trialled the search terms, sought feedback on them by posting them on our research blog (though did not receive any) and assessed the number, type and spread of 'hits' that they generated as part of our pilot study. A protocol is an important part of the pilot. As we trialled search terms, we developed a protocol that captured critical details and which the two of us could use independently and together as we tackled these issues. What we were seeking was a balance between achieving sufficient data and a necessary focus on topic (the trade-off between breadth and depth). That means running the pilot for long enough to be able to see likely trends; in our case, as noted above, this was four weeks. For full details of our pilot study see Pritchard and Whiting (2012a). Time can be limited on a Masters research project, hence our advice that using qualitative Internet data needs good planning just as much as other methods of data collection such as interview or survey studies. In Chapter 4 we provide practical suggestions for how to conduct a pilot study as well as some guidance for the researcher who really does not have time to do so before starting their data collection.

A key issue to bear in mind when piloting is the transitory and dynamic nature of many web sources. For example, we found in the course of piloting that there was an optimum time point at which to collect comments on online newspaper articles. If we downloaded the article too soon after its initial publication online there might only be a handful of below-the-line reader comments; too long after publication and comments might have been closed or removed. In this case, downloading between three and ten days after publication provided the best result in terms of maximizing the data (Pritchard and Whiting, 2012a, 2014). The pilot study presents a good opportunity to check practical issues about the frequency and timing of data capture as well as to reflect on more broadly, and review where necessary, all aspects of the data collection method.

The pilot is also a chance to assess if the proposed data management system is fit for purpose (that is, whether it keeps the data in a stable form, maintains data security, complies with various legal and ethical requirements, enables data search, retrieval and analysis as well as anticipating potential publication). This includes getting to grips with any CAQDAS package that the researcher has decided to use. Until the pilot study starts, the researcher will be largely unaware of how many 'hits' are going to be returned on a daily basis. Their first task will be to review, say, the first days or week of the pilot to determine how they might process the data and utilize their selected data management system. The starting point is assessing relevance, does the 'hit' fit the scope of the project? If no, discard as data. If yes, then it becomes data to be incorporated into the project. If using a CAQDAS package, this will involve incorporating the data into the project software database. This might be a simple upload where the data type is supported and the database allows direct import (such as NVivo allowing direct import of certain types of social media data). If the data form is not supported, the researcher may need to convert the data in a way that makes it compatible with upload. If not using a CAQDAS package, then the researcher will need to convert the data into a stable form and save it within a folder structure that will enable subsequent data search, retrieval and analysis.

The pilot also offers the chance to consider ethical issues more closely. We found that once we were actually handling data in the pilot study, we had a much better idea of the forms of data that would be generated in our project and what the related ethical issues might be. The pilot provided a tangible basis (and examples of data) for our discussions. It had been difficult for us as researchers and our institutional ethics officers/committee to assess these issues in advance. This is somewhat easier now due to the increase in specialist advice and guidelines regarding the ethical considerations of Internet research (see examples in Table 3.2 above) but is still not straightforward. In our case, we needed to develop flexible ethical guidelines that would enable us to respond to the data generated throughout the project. This meant ethics was an ongoing process rather than a one-off tick box exercise at the outset of the project, requiring us to build in further ethical reviews at each stage (Pritchard and Whiting, 2012a). As we have flagged in the section on ethics above, researchers will need to work with the guidelines and procedures at their institutions to ensure ethical compliance; this may require a review once the pilot study is completed.

Overall, the pilot study is a good opportunity for reflexivity in the decision-making process. This is the time to reflect on how things have worked and make any necessary changes. Unlike, say, interviews where a researcher can ask the pilot study participant for feedback on the questions, the researcher in a qualitative Internet data study is more dependent on their own reflections, though for Master students these can be usefully discussed with their project supervisors. Taking comprehensive notes of what is done and why certain choices have been made will be invaluable in writing up the methods chapter of a Masters research dissertation. This level of detail and reflexivity enables a full consideration of justifying and critiquing the methodology as we discuss in Chapter 6.

CONDUCTING THE MAIN STUDY

Assuming the researcher has followed the pointers that we have outlined so far in this chapter, including carrying out and reflecting on a pilot study, then actually conducting the main study should in many ways be relatively straightforward. Most of the difficult decisions have been taken and the details and mechanics of data collection are by now tried and tested. However, it is worth noting that even with having conducted a pilot study, the researcher is unlikely to achieve a 'perfect' qualitative Internet research design. More likely what they have determined is a workable way forward for the rest of their research project. This should include building in regular sense checks and points at which they can review and discuss progress with their supervisor as a means of ensuring that issues arising can be re-considered and addressed as required.

One of the key issues is likely to relate to determining when enough data has been collected (and see our comments above regarding sample size). From a practical perspective, many Masters research projects will have timescales that prevent extending the period of data collection in order for the researcher to have time to analyse the data and write up the dissertation. One advantage of the qualitative Internet studies, however, is that data collection is ongoing and largely automated; analysis can start as soon as the first tranche of data has been downloaded; the collection period can easily be extended without involving the researcher in more work (cf. interviews) so that collection and analysis can run simultaneously where necessary.

DATA MANAGEMENT AND PREPARING FOR ANALYSIS

The scope of this book is focused on data collection. However, we appreciate that data analysis is a key stage in any research project, so we set out here some key pointers for the management of qualitative Internet data in readiness for subsequent analysis. Often there is little scope during a pilot study to analyse this initial data though the researcher will have needed to conduct a quick read of the material generated by the alerts etc. to assess for relevance. A key aim of the pilot is to ensure that the data management structures are in place for the researcher to be able to search, retrieve and analyse the data. In the main study, data management should be fairly easy to maintain if the researcher has set up structures and systems along the lines discussed earlier. The challenge is that the researcher is now working with substantial volumes of data that need to be transformed before analysis can take place. This is common across different types of qualitative research (Richards, 2009). Qualitative Internet research is no exception though the steps and transformations required are different to, say, those in an interview or survey study.

In all cases, raw data are converted into a research artefact, which then needs to be managed before it can be analysed. The pilot study will hopefully have enabled the researcher to develop a suitable data management system (one that keeps the data in a stable form, maintains data security, complies with the various legal and ethical requirements, and enables data search, retrieval and analysis). Depending on data types and volume, budget and time constraints, the management system might involve CAQDAS or might be limited to using standard office software on a secure password protected computer. In either case, the key aim is to make it easier to conduct the data analysis. This involves identifying patterns in the data and assessing the data against theoretical and empirical concepts in a way that both addresses the research question(s) and, in doing so, generates a contribution to knowledge and understanding of the topic. So, the management system needs to be able to accommodate ways of searching the data (which might be in multiple formats) and recording the different stages in the analysis, including notes and coding that the researcher generates. If not using specialist software, then typically this might involve logging data items into a spreadsheet, having a structure of (electronic) folders for different data types or cases and using different coloured highlighting to indicate coding.

There are many different methods of qualitative analysis. Some are consistent with particular research philosophies (for example, discourse analysis is consistent with a social constructionist perspective); some (such as **thematic analysis**) are flexible and can be used with a variety of different epistemological and ontological positions. But in all cases, analysis is a lengthy iterative process of many stages where keeping good records through a data management system will make the subsequent dissertation write up much easier. As part of the overall data management, the researcher is advised to keep a **research diary** of their analysis enabling them to capture their thoughts about the data at each stage in the process. Recording patterns that the researcher observes, how these fit together, how these link to existing theoretical, conceptual and empirical work and how they address the project research question(s) is a key part of the analytic process. A good system of data management will help the researcher to record these stages and find data examples, which will be invaluable in writing up the project dissertation.

CHAPTER SUMMARY

In this chapter, we have:

- set out the basic components of tracking and trawling
- provided details of what is required at each stage in preparing for and collecting qualitative digital data using the tracking and trawling methods
- highlighted the ethical considerations of qualitative Internet data
- explained the importance of conducting a pilot study.

We have illustrated these stages with examples from our own research and fictional student projects. We have also cross-referred to aspects that we look at in more detail in Chapter 5 as part of our consideration of published studies which have used these methods. Our aim here has been to flag the key issues to consider at each of these stages. In the next chapter, we offer more detailed guidance as the researcher begins to grapple with the practicalities of collecting online research data.

4

CONDUCTING RESEARCH ONLINE

INTRODUCTION

This chapter offers guidance for collecting online data. We first focus on the practicalities of research and address issues that might be encountered irrespective of whether the approach is tracking or trawling, or indeed a combination of the two. Having reviewed many of the practical issues associated with collecting online data we then move to consider more complex considerations related to researching online.

The following topics are reviewed in this chapter:

* maintaining focus on the research question
* practical issues of a pilot
* managing tools and technology
* are these data?
* balancing acts: opportunity vs overwhelming
* getting ready for analysis.

MAINTAINING FOCUS ON THE RESEARCH QUESTION

As with all types of research project, it is important to be clear on the aims and objectives of the investigation. At the start of the last chapter we covered the process of designing research questions. Here we deal with the practicalities of **monitoring** and even **revising the research question** as data collection proceeds.

Confirming the Research Question

At the start of any research, there needs to be a process of test and challenge regarding the research question(s) posed. The most common ways in which this is undertaken include:

- discussion with a research collaborator or supervisor
- review of a research proposal
- comparison with the literature.

It is likely that any (or all) of these processes will provide useful feedback on the practical aspects of research. However, with online research there can also be a virtual process of test and challenge. While this will vary depending on the actual research focus, a common approach is to undertake a generic web search of the research question, either in its entirety or breaking down the question into its key components. The examples provided in Chapters 2 and 3 all highlight the different ways in which this can proceed. Below we focus on one of our previous examples and break this down in more detail.

In Chapter 2 (Box 2.1), we introduced the example of Mia and her research on diversity and social media. If we take Mia's research question as an example (How do UK financial institutions use social media to communicate their commitment to diversity?) and simply conduct a Google search, this highlights many useful sources of information from actors such as the **Bank of England**, the **Building Societies Association** and **British Bankers Association**. While it can be tempting to wait and see if such resources may be part of the dataset, it is important to engage with relevant contextual information during this test and challenge process. This will help ensure that the research question is targeting the topic in a meaningful way in relation to the area to be explored. Reading background materials related to the research topic that are already in the public domain can therefore enable a good understanding of the way in which different subjects are framed and become familiar with practitioner language.

Relatedly there is increasing recognition of the importance of the so-called **grey literature** in shaping research projects (Adams et al., 2017). The term grey literature refers to material that is not published commercially or subject to the most rigorous standards of academic review. This can include reports and documents produced by many different types of organizations across the private, public and third sectors. Whereas once access to such material required direct contact with an organization and a physical product, such sources are now widely available online. As mentioned above, this may present a dilemma for researchers who need to decide whether such material is included as part of the literature review or features as online data. This decision will depend on the approach and focus of the particular research question. Indeed, in most cases there will not be a clear cut answer so it is important to ensure a rationale is developed and consistently applied during the research. Consideration of the grey literature in research in many fields is an emergent concern and consulting the latest debates relevant to the topic will be important in determining the approach (Adams et al., 2017).

Once the parameters are confirmed and the initial search conducted, the materials need to be selected that will be used to provide the test and challenge. Again, the way in which this is carried out will likely be determined by the particular topic of investigation. However, this might include consideration of:

- **Key actors** that operate in relation to the topic. In the example of Mia above (and Chapter 2), clearly the views of the major banking institutions and regulators would provide a useful understanding. In the case of Belinda (Chapter 3), she may want to consider those organizations involved in health and safety regulation for kitchen work.
- Identifying and engaging with **alternative perspectives** to the major players. In Mia's example looking at a relevant diversity campaign (such as Stonewall) might provide a useful alternative view.

As with all research, looking at methods papers in relevant journals and empirical studies with similar approaches, even if the topics are different, can also provide useful insights into this stage of research. We cover examples in further detail in Chapter 5. Depending on the context of the research project, consulting key stakeholders including any sponsors of the research will also be important at this stage.

Monitoring and Revising the Research Question

While a review of the research question before starting data collection offers a relatively contained approach to test and challenge, ensuring this continues through the data collection process is more difficult. This is particularly so in the case of online research. In many approaches to qualitative research, the researcher is directly interacting with participants during the shared construction of the dataset. This provides a space for ongoing reflexive engagement with the research question during the research process. An overview of reflexivity is provided in Chapters 1 and 2 and, as with any qualitative research undertaking, consider the overall approach to reflexivity across all phases of the research.

During the processes of tracking and trawling that we describe in this book, the focus is largely on collecting material that has been posted online in one form or another. It is true that some material takes a **dialogic form**, for example:

- **exchanges between individuals** during an online discussion forum
- various means of developing **threads of comments** on social media such as Twitter, which may include visual responses such as **memes** (Milner, 2016)
- comments (and comments on comments) in **below-the-line sections** in online media and via social media such as Twitter.

As highlighted in Chapter 2, we recognize that researchers engage more directly in some methods such as online ethnography (Hine, 2008) or netnography (Kozinets et al., 2014) in which there is a focus on a particular online community. Kozinets and colleagues state that netnographic research 'requires an initial and deepening cultural understanding of the community' (2014: 266). However, in tracking and trawling the researcher is usually further removed from a particular community and adopts an observer stance to online activity. This means that the process of ongoing reflexivity must be actively managed to ensure that the focus and relevance of the research question is maintained.

This might be achieved in a number of ways, including:

- Maintaining a research diary that allows for reflexive note taking on the process of data collection. A private blog could be used for this.
- Undertaking a '**snapshot**' review of the material being collected. Depending on the form of data collection this might involve a random selection of ten items of data or a single day's data collection. Using this data as a prompt, record initial reactions and the ways in which this data relates to the research question. Repeating this process at regular intervals allows monitoring and consideration of adjustments to search processes.
- Attending seminars or **research training** to share research or listen to others and reflect these experiences back onto the research question.

In much qualitative research, rather than being completely fixed at the outset, the research question(s) will evolve during the process of data collection. What is important here is that this evolution is, as far as possible, managed in a reflexive way. This usually involves going between the data that is being collected and the original research question to consider whether there is any need to change or adjust the research question, data collection approaches, or indeed both. One of the advantages of many approaches to collecting online data is that it is relatively easy to adapt or adjust these, for example by adding additional search terms or broadening the scope of sources under consideration.

PRACTICAL ISSUES OF A PILOT

As we have discussed elsewhere (Pritchard and Whiting, 2012a), pilot tests are rarely discussed in depth in the qualitative research literature. Although more openly discussed in research seminars and conference presentations, many explorative forays and confirmatory processes with the research process remain largely hidden from view. Those who are able to talk with other qualitative researchers, are often able to tap into a rich vein of insights into the false starts, hiccups, recalibrations and serendipitous events that shape empirical undertakings. Classically, Denzin and Lincoln (1994: 201) refer to explorations that 'parallel the warm-up exercise and cool down periods of dance'.

As explored within Chapter 3 it is important to define the parameters of pilot test-ing. This may involve a degree of pragmatism as time and resources often constrain the scope and extent of pilot testing. Undertaking a review of the key research steps and using some form of RAG (red, amber, green) or traffic light assessment can help decide which elements to focus on. For example, the following criteria could be applied:

- How do I rate my experience in this step?
- How reliable are the tools to perform this step?
- How critical is this step to the overall research project?
- How easy will it be to repeat or correct this step?
- How much existing methodological guidance do I have access to for this step?

As outlined in Chapter 3, once the pilot parameters are defined, a clear protocol for how to conduct the pilot should be developed. This should include a view on how to assess the results. For online research it is usual to pilot the search procedure to be used in tracking and/or trawling. Typically, this will involve a series of limited 'dry runs'. In this regard the retrospective focus of trawling is somewhat more straight-forward than the future orientation of tracking. In a tracking study, particularly if designed to follow an anticipated or scheduled event, it is less easy to predict how or where data may occur. It might also be difficult to find an alternative, related event for a pilot. In such cases then it is important to closely monitor the first days of the live data collection.

Additionally, it is important to identify any particularly high-risk or difficult aspects of the research design that need to be tested. For instance, where data collection is scheduled for a short timeframe by following a specific time-bound one-off event (such as the reporting of annual results), the pilot should include a test within a similar timeframe. In some cases, it may be possible to use a similar previous event as a pilot case study. As an illustration, to study the way in which marketing across social media links and adapts to events at a sporting tournament such as the **FIFA Women's World Cup**, it would be possible to use trawling during the pilot to explore a previous tournament.

With online research, the pilot should also assess the ways in which the techno-logical set up might shape or influence data collection. This is further discussed in the section below on managing tools and technology, however, wherever possible it is important to replicate the main study approach during pilot testing. In the case where Google searches are to be used as part of tracking and trawling approaches, it is important to be aware that location plays a part in determining search results. This means that if a search query is entered in French, but the IP address is located in Wales then the search results return will prioritize links for that location and in English (not Welsh or French!). Understanding the way in which settings can be adjusted and tailored to impact the way in which the tools chosen will work is a key part of the pilot testing process.

While conducting the pilot is of course important, it is how the results are assessed that will impact the shape of further research. At the start of a qualitative research endeavour it is usual to be concerned that we may not obtain enough rich data. Across a range of methods, piloting is often undertaken to ensure we feel confident that sufficient data of good quality will be obtained. Both quantity and quality are therefore important measures to consider and the assessment of these will be impacted by the type of data collected and the approach by which these data will be analysed.

With online research methods, however, it is particularly important to consider how to deal with too much data, and indeed what this might entail. This is particularly relevant to individual and time-limited research projects, such as a Masters dissertation. A pilot test can alert the researcher to the likely challenges associated with a large quantity of data and allow time to experiment with different strategies for addressing these.

It is important to remember that all research will have limitations, it is not possible to research everything and setting clear boundaries for data collections is critical to the success of the project. At this stage it is important to write down the boundaries decided for the research going forward, the decisions taken about these and the way in which this will impact research findings. Commonly in online qualitative data collections the key decisions will relate to:

- data types
- data sources
- **data variables** (such as language and country of origin)
- **timeframes for data collection** (including length of data collection and frequency of sampling within this timespan)
- **platforms used**.

Later in this chapter we reflect further on revisiting these decisions when there is a need to further restrict or extend the dataset.

Pilot testing also provides an opportunity to consider how data will be practically handled and this requires designing and testing a set of protocols for data management. The specifics of this will vary depending on the types of data and analysis plans but most include some form of download protocol. Testing this with anticipated data sources and types, so far as possible within the scope of the pilot, will help ensure data collection is complete and metadata are also recorded. Metadata in tracking and trawling includes the identifying information related to the particular online source (such as URL), dates posted (and potentially updated), any author or origin data related to the source (and component aspects such as images). Figure 4.1 provides a marked-up example (from our own blog), which shows what metadata might be of interest, while Table 4.1 shows how these would be captured in this case.

Figure 4.1 Source example

Table 4.1 Record for source example

Data reference including identification/download references	Source type and URL or similar	Log of item details	Item content and data storage
0001 (a unique reference)	Blog post	Title: New methods book underway!	Text of blog post (18 lines)
From: Google search	Ageatwork.wordpress.com		
On: 14/10/19 10.40 work PC		Author: Katrina Pritchard	No additional data downloaded.
Downloaded: same time.		Publication date: 14/10/19	Storage: Project USB

If it is not possible to undertake a full pilot test of the data analytic processes, then the following questions provide useful prompts for a paper-based review:

- What is it I have found: details of the data source, any identifying information?
- How I found this: process of identification (particularly important if multiple collection strategies are being used or where additional snowballing is employed).
- What does this data look like: a description of the data?
- What elements are there: the components that will form the basis of analysis?
- What else is here that I am not going to collect: such as deciding not to download embedded adverts?

Building on our example from earlier, Figures 4.2 and Table 4.2 now show how this additional information might be captured within an extended data log. Note that for ease of presentation the earlier information shown in Figure 4.1 and Table 4.1 has been removed. A full detailed log is, however, recommended.

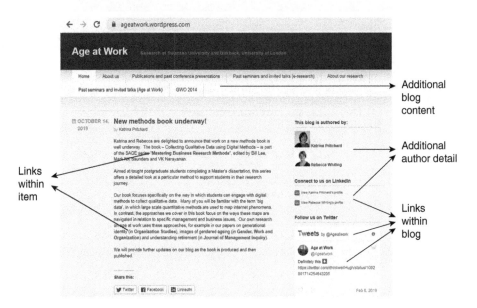

Figure 4.2   Source example with additional information noted

Table 4.2   Additional record for source example

Data reference including identification/ download references	Source full log	Item full log	Notes
0001 (a unique reference) From: Google search On: 14/10/19 10.40 work PC Downloaded: same time.	WordPress blog containing six tables, rolling blog posts and side bar. Additional tabs not reviewed. Sidebar contains author images (not downloaded). Sidebar links: Author LinkedIn profiles (not reviewed). Twitter account @ ageatwork (not reviewed). Tweets embedded.	Text of blog post (18 lines). No embedded images or other media. Four embedded links, all reviewed and itemized, see data items: 0002 0003 0004 0005	The blog post is a news type post consisting of four short paragraphs. Embedded links have been reviewed and downloaded as separate data items. No additional follow up required.

In our own research (Pritchard and Whiting, 2012a) we reflect on key challenges of the pilot test. First, at this early stage of the research process it is likely to encounter issues that, with more experience at a later stage, may not have been labelled as issues at all. This may cause delays to the research process and seeking advice from a supervisor or research colleague can prove invaluable. Indeed, using the pilot to develop 'problem-solving' approaches can be as valuable as using a pilot to 'solve problems'. The second is the importance of recognizing when the research process is 'good enough'. There will be no perfect process and, especially when working to a particular timeframe, spending too long procrastinating in the pilot stage may mean less time for later analytic stages to the detriment of overall research contribution. However, the forward thinking process of piloting provides an invaluable opportunity 'to be reflexive about how the research will develop in the future' (Pritchard and Whiting, 2012a: 350).

MANAGING TOOLS AND TECHNOLOGY

Issues related to managing tools and technology vary widely depending on the specifics of the research project and level of experience with the different technologies involved. To some extent, the tools and technologies deployed will depend on the focus of the research project. Exploring previously published research will help in spotting trends in this regard. However, when researching the advantages and disadvantages of different tools, factoring in practical considerations like cost, accessibility and skill level is also essential. There are now many (online) reviews available of the various platforms that might be used in online research and assessments of the protocols and search tools (a sample is provided below).

As we have highlighted elsewhere in this book, the tools and technology that are used in data collection are not neutral. Rather, these shape the data. Here we are not going to examine the various platform algorithms but, as explored in depth by Pearce and colleagues (2018), note the importance of carefully considering the implications of platform choice. It is important to bear in mind that the ways in which online data are created and accessed are continuously evolving. Pritchard's (2020) research has involved collecting images which related to contemporary work concepts. She has primarily used **Google image search** for these projects and over the last five years has noted that the way in which the search results are displayed, the options provided for filtering results and the suggestions made for related images have changed each year. For this reason, it is really important to review (and note) the processes currently being used in data collection.

A further challenge when collecting online data is the ever-evolving range of tools and technologies available. As with the student examples provided throughout this book it is important to relate the types of technology chosen to the research question, for example:

- Mia (Box 2.1) Twitter and Instagram via subject.
- Jakob (Box 2.2) online news (specific type).
- Charlie (Box 2.3) Twitter via hashtags.
- Henny (Box 2.4) online news.
- Alywyn (Box 2.5) social media as a gateway to online course details.
- Gwen (Box 2.6) Twitter and Instagram.

These examples use well-established tools and are therefore manageable for a Masters research project. However, it is important to note that new tools may also be considered. For example, the emergence of **live streaming** via apps such as Periscope has added a new dimension to social media use (Stewart and Littau, 2016). Additionally, there is a whole host of APIs (**Application Programming Interfaces**) that provide means to access a range of social media data. Often these are used in sophisticated ways as part of big data projects that extend beyond the scope of this book.

It is important to remember that, particularly in the wake of the **Cambridge Analytica** and Facebook scandal (Atefeh and Khreich, 2015), accessibility and use of data are being more closely scrutinized. Because of the closed status of Facebook, we regard this as one of the most problematic sites for academic research despite its popularity across a range of academic fields (Stoycheff et al., 2017). Of the other social media sites, Twitter has proved one of the most popular while a variety of research uses data accessed from other online media, blogs and sites such as Reddit and Mumsnet.

Above, we focus primarily on text, however, the visual in online research is increasingly recognized as of critical importance (Miltner and Highfield, 2017). In tracking and trawling studies, there is a focus on non-participatory visual studies, that is to say, the images are not prompted in response to the researcher (Pritchard, 2020). For this reason, sites such as Instagram and YouTube are of particular interest for online research. However, the visual online is a complex mix of pre-existing and emerging visualization trends, many of which are themselves technologically facilitated. Terms such as selfie, **GIF** and meme (Miltner and Highfield, 2017) denote new visual forms while digital manipulation techniques are now widely in use. If the research project involves the collection of visual data, it is important to consider how and why a whole variety of different forms might be collected. Chapter 5 provides examples of many different types of data.

For those interested in exploring further information on tools, below (Box 4.1) we highlight resources on different aspects of digital methods.

Box 4.1   Additional Information

Emerald Publishing Guide: www.emeraldgrouppublishing.com/research/guides/management/digital_technology.htm

This is an introductory site that provides some general guidelines on social media use in research and by researchers. Discussing the social sciences more broadly, there is a review of the ways in which digital technology has changed research and further links to a range of resources.

Social Media Data Stewardship, Ryerson University, Canada: https://socialmediadata.org/

This site covers a range of social media and pays particular attention to ethics. There are specific resources for researchers on data collection, storage, analysis, publishing, sharing and preservation.

LSE Guide on Social Media Research: https://blogs.lse.ac.uk/impactofsocialsciences/2019/06/18/using-twitter-as-a-data-source-an-overview-of-social-media-research-tools-2019/

Regularly updated, this site reviews data collection approaches across a range of social media. There is a clear review of tools that can be used for different social media sites and many useful links.

The following academic papers provide excellent summaries of particular platforms:

On Twitter:

Mollett, A., Moran, D., and Dunleavy, P. (2011). *Using Twitter in University Research, Teaching and Impact Activities.* Impact of social sciences: Maximizing the impact of academic research. LSE Public Policy Group. London: London School of Economics and Political Science. This version available at: http://eprints.lse.ac.uk/38489/

On Instagram:

Highfield, T. and Leaver, T. (2016). Instagrammatics and digital methods: Studying visual social media, from selfies and GIFs to memes and emoji. *Communication Research and Practice, 2*(1), 47-62.

On YouTube:

Shifman, L. (2012). An anatomy of a YouTube meme. *New Media & Society, 14*(2), 187-203.

Overall:

Snelson, C. L. (2016). Qualitative and mixed methods social media research: A review of the literature. *International Journal of Qualitative Methods, 15*(1), https://doi.org/10.1177/1609406915624574.

Alongside academic research, there is booming market for **bespoke qualitative online research**, particularly for market, consumer and opinion research. Most of these products are costly and their use in academic settings is not well established. Furthermore, many of these tools facilitate online data collection directly from participants. However, these participants are not already online but are recruited for the specific purposes of a research project. We would therefore suggest a cautious approach to such products.

Given the above, it is not surprising that many researchers begin their forays into online research using the tools that they are already familiar with. Indeed, it may also be tempting to use an existing social media or email account as a tool within research. This is something to weigh up carefully. One of the disadvantages of using personal accounts is that it may be difficult to separate other work and even personal use from the research project, and the volume of data related content might become overwhelming. On the other hand, managing all work from one account may be a personal preference and many offer filtering tools that can help manage this. Whatever accounts are used, it is important to consider whether previous device or account usage may impact the tracking and trawling undertaken. It is advisable to use the private or anonymous settings available on some tools and/or to clear browser data before conducting specific data collection tasks. If using an alert or monitoring tool as part of data collection, then it is important to ensure you understand how searches are performed and the ways in which this might shape the data sources within the alert. One of the most popular tools, Google Alerts, works best with news sources and webpages (such as blogs) but does not cover social media data such as Twitter. Pilot testing tools is an important step in ensuring that alerts are delivering useful content for the research project.

From a practical perspective, the security of personal data and research data also needs careful consideration. During our early online research, we encountered several **rogue websites** that promoted malware and prompted us to ensure our own devices were adequately protected. It is important to seek expert technical advice on this issue. Depending on the research topic, this may be more or less of a risk with online research. The most appropriate course of action will be tailored to the particular technology in use, ensuring devices are fully protected with appropriate security software.

According to the tools used and research protocols, it is of course important to consider how research will proceed in case of any access disruption. Service interruptions may impact the dataset and a decision will be needed as to whether to take action to plug any gaps, through re-running particular search protocols. If the research relates to a particular time period or event, then it is important to consider this issue in advance and include a contingency plan within a piloting protocol.

ARE THESE DATA?

Qualitative data are often defined by what they are not: **numeric**. Interrogating what qualitative data are is a more complex affair. It is also dynamic. We might initially draw a comparison between quantitative data collected from many individuals via a survey instrument and qualitative data collected from fewer individuals via direct research engagement, via interview (Cassell, 2015) or focus groups (Oates and Alevizou, 2017). However, this does not reflect the diversity of data types and sources available online for either quantitative or qualitative researchers.

In terms of tracking and/or trawling, as we discuss in Chapter 1, we are referring to textual and/or visual non-numeric data that are collected online. As we discussed in the previous section on tools and technologies, these data are enormously variable and multi-modal. Invoking the term multi-modal here recognizes not just that there are different forms or types of data but that the relationships between these are complex. In smaller scale research projects, it is often necessary to focus on a particular mode, or at least give primacy to the relationship between one mode and a limited number of others. In more extensive studies, beyond the scope of a student dissertation, there is opportunity to fully engage with the complexity of multi-modality. However, it is important to note that online studies in business and management have been at the vanguard of tackling the challenge of multi-modality, as we explore in Chapter 5.

When conducting a tracking and/or trawling study it is highly likely that many different types of data will be encountered. However, the circulation of these data presents a further challenge. In our own research we often encounter the same 'story' (usually a construction of text and visual images) across many different online sites and social media. Most of the time it is relatively straightforward to identify the origin, especially when these can be traced to organizational press releases or similar public announcements. We are helped in this by the nature of our topic (age at work) and our familiarity with the key actors and organizations that participate in many online debates. However, despite this familiarity it is still possible to be surprised by the apparent unprompted repeat of a story or reawakening of a debate on social media, some months after its first appearance. This might involve a historical press release being picked up by online media or the resurfacing and sharing of a previous social media post. The extent to which this matters to a research project will depend on the way in which timing and temporality are positioned in respect to the research question posed. If an event focus is adopted, then it might be important to determine if the data collected relates to that specific occurrence of the event. In other studies, the date of origin of the offline event that prompted online discussion may not be relevant.

We have also noted the disappearance of data. Most commonly this was encountered when reviewing alert or search results and following the link provided to the source. Sometimes the source had been moved, deleted or changed from what was noted. This is simply part of the challenge of collecting online data and highlights the importance of reviewing content as it is identified by the particular digital tools in use.

Advanced studies may include a consideration of the flow of topics across different online media. Flow may encompass both quantitative and qualitative aspects of how stories and items translate across different platforms and media and such metadata are important to consider at the start of the research project. This is, however, a more advanced approach that requires a very tightly defined research question and a clear strategy of how to track particular online media. Because of the advanced nature of such a research project it is not recommended for a Masters research project.

In Chapter 2 we highlighted that issues of authenticity and fakery are often raised in online research. In some cases, the originators of data may be specific and clearly identifiable by username or tag. However, these online identities may not be themselves traceable to a particular individual. In other cases, the identity of contributors may be (either deliberately or otherwise) obscured.

In nearly all of our research presentations over the last ten years, some form of the following question has been asked:

> Is what you are collecting really data? Surely, it is just 'stuff' people have posted online and it might not be true. You often don't know who has posted something or why.

From one perspective we would argue that this statement is true for a whole range of both quantitative and qualitative research methods. Indeed, this is a debate that has engaged academics across a range of disciplines for many years and goes to the heart of epistemology. Our response to this question across all our joint and separate research projects has been that we are inherently interested in this 'stuff' and particularly in what this tells us about the processes of social construction. We go further and suggest that given the prominence of the Internet and social media in our lives, attending to this 'stuff' is essential.

Unpacking this further, a research project may involve a trawling study investigating sustainability, similar to the case of Henny in Chapter 2. Taking this example further, let us assume that a research project has a broader scope than Henny's automotive sector focus and involves comparing across a range of company types. In this example, the case of a double-glazing company is selected for a pilot study, which starts with a review of the double-glazing company website. This contains pages about products including claims on energy efficiency, details about the business including awards won in recent years, links to press coverage of the firm and testimonials from satisfied customers. There is a mix of text, image and video embedded in the website which also references Instagram, Facebook and Twitter accounts. As the search broadens, the researcher finds that the adverts and promotions featuring double glazing from this organization have started to appear on their own social media feed. These feature information about price and sales offers, rather than the sustainability focus of the website. In this case, the researcher might start to wonder whether the sustainability discourse of the website reflects the organization at all. The direction of this wondering will of course depend on the ontological and epistemological underpinning of the research project. For a post-positivist approach, this might be seen as a particular use of different channels for different messages and different audiences. For an interpretivist, it may lead to an examination of the way in which the company is making sense of the customer and their interests, whereas a more critical project might interrogate the discursive construction of sustainability and the potential impact of greenwashing. All of these approaches would still regard this as data. Messy data yes, but pretty much all data are messy until we process them through an analytical frame.

BALANCING ACTS: OPPORTUNITY VS OVERWHELMING

The bounty of online data is a key attraction for those undertaking tracking and trawling approaches. However, such bounty may also prove to be problematic. It is important to recognize that this bounty is not simply a question of quantity, although this may also be a factor. Additionally, however, the increasing richness of online data means that the bounty is also one of quality.

During our research we have usually closely monitored the early stages of data collection, regularly scanning the material collected and reviewing at a high level. This high-level review involved an overview of the volume of material identified, the key features and sources. As covered above, this monitoring involved considering these data in relation to the research questions for our study. As a result of these reviews we could decide on adjustments to either the data collection processes or refining the research questions, or on occasion both. In making adjustments to the data collection processes, there were two key criteria employed:

- Would the adjustment reduce the quantity of redundant data?
- Would the adjustment result in additional relevant data being identified?

Whenever an adjustment was made to the data collection processes, the subsequent few days of data collection would be closely monitored to review the outcomes.

It is often difficult to contemplate reducing the scale of data collection during a study. However, it is important to bear in mind that data collection must be manageable for the resources available for the project. Below we discuss how a dataset might be managed in the preparation for analysis, but during data collection there is the opportunity to review and revise in 'real time'. The way in which this is managed will largely depend on the research focus but a simple distinction between data that are 'need to have' rather than 'nice to have' is a good place to start. This assessment can be incorporated within a pilot but often requires the realization of volume to prompt action. The most common methods deployed to filter data include:

- Using popularity as a criterion for inclusion. This is particularly relevant where social media posts can be ranked according to likes or shares.
- Selecting a structured sample across media types (e.g. drawing data from different social media platforms, which could involve selecting based on recency from different sites).
- Selecting a structured sample based across the different search terms or hashtags used.

Within Chapter 5 we provide several examples of the application of different strategies in research projects. Overall, we have found that both tracking and trawling studies often start with relatively broad search protocols, often because of a fear of missing out. However, careful review during both a pilot and the early stages of data collection can help target protocols (using the pointers in the list above) to ensure data collection is effective and manageable.

It is important not to assume that data will be bountiful, however. It may be that the research question is particularly targeted or covers a niche area. The broader search approach adopted in many studies may be problematic in these cases. Here a pilot will be essential, but even approaches that work during a pilot may not subsequently work sufficiently during a longer study given the way in which topics of debate come and go online. In such cases it is very useful to deploy online snowballing techniques to follow sources and links from within the initial source identified, so identifying further data. These types of focused projects can also provide the opportunity to extend the modalities under consideration and combine different tracking and trawling methods.

GETTING READY FOR ANALYSIS

The thorny question of how much data are enough data for a qualitative research project is always difficult to answer. If the research question relates to a particular event or timeframe, clear parameters may have been determined at the start of the research project. Indeed, given the intended audience for this book, it is very likely that the deadlines may have been set in the guise of a project deadline. Nevertheless, it is always difficult to draw a close to data collection, even more so in methods like tracking and trawling since the researcher may feel a less than active participant than in, say, an interview study (see the earlier discussion on saturation in Chapter 3). In that sense it is important to ensure that a monitoring process follows alongside the tracking and trawling and that automated search or alert processes are reviewed during data collection, using the approaches of logging sources highlighted in Figures 4.1 and 4.2 and Tables 4.1 and 4.2.

This monitoring will allow ongoing review of the progress towards being able to answer the research question and therefore allow a clearer judgement to be made of when to move forward with data analysis. Of course, one of the many advantages of automated online search processes and tools is that these can often be left to run in the background afterwards.

However, at some point it is essential to decide on the dataset to be used in a particular project. This decision will be shaped by the research question and analytic approach, as well as pragmatic issues such as time and capability. For example, a research project that encompasses multi-modal data is very likely to require a focus on a smaller dataset given the complexity of the analytic process. Similarly, a tracking study that began with a broad range of voices to follow online, could well need to focus on a smaller number if the volume of data collected exceeds expectations. An overview of the approaches of focusing during data collection are listed in the previous section. As discussed in Chapter 3, a continual review of data to determine if saturation has been reached is another strategy adopted by some researchers (Boland, 2016). Ultimately all these decisions often involve a trade-off between breadth and depth and will benefit from some 'what if?' analyses to guide decision-making. As we prepare for analysis, we have often used mind-mapping to help us through these decisions, working with the research question at the centre and mapping the alternative datasets against these. These can then be reviewed during the data analysis stage to adjust and fine tune the dataset if the initial parameters prove problematic

However, some authors (Breitbarth et al., 2010) suggest refraining from making any adjustments to the size of the dataset until an initial stage of analysis. At this stage, cases or sub-sets of data can then be selected for further analysis. It is sensible to consult previous studies in the relevant area and appropriate analytic methodology to distil advice on how to proceed at this stage. Whichever approach is selected, it is important to clearly note the decisions taken and how this impacted the resulting dataset. This audit trail is considered essential for judgements of quality in qualitative research. Discussing and reviewing this decision-making with a research supervisor or peers is also strongly advised.

The work of getting ready for analysis will depend on the extent to which data were processed during collection. In our early research, which followed a tracking approach, we collected data over many months. We began with a clearly defined pilot (Pritchard and Whiting, 2012a), which not only looked at the data collected but at how we would download sources and what metadata would be recorded. At that time there were fewer tools available to facilitate the downloading of online data so for many web sources we were simply cutting and pasting. A lesson learnt early at this stage was that our initial design of a template using a word table for each day proved problematic for later analysis. Indeed, we had to do further work to remove the table formatting to be able to proceed with analysis. Depending on the choice of tools and technology (see Chapter 3 and earlier in this chapter) there are now many ways of automating the data downloading process. Each of these should be thoroughly tested during the design of the pilot.

It is highly likely that whatever monitoring processes have been undertaken (see earlier in this chapter), the first step at the end of the data collection phase will be one of data clean up. It is easy to underestimate the time and effort that this will take. One of the advantages of online research which collects pre-existing materials is exactly that they exist in a form that seems readily amenable to analysis. However, there is usually a significant amount of work to be undertaken which may include:

- Removing irrelevant or **redundant items**: in our original research on age at work, we used the key words 'generation' and 'work' in a tracking study aimed at exploring the way in which different generational cohorts were positioned at work. However, these terms also returned many items related to new models of car, which were clearly not relevant to our research questions and so were ignored and not collected.
- Dealing with **repeat items**: for some research questions, the repeat items will be 'noise' and can simply be removed. This is of course the most straightforward course of action and, when there is a tight research brief or timescale, this is likely to be the most pragmatic option. However, in some projects repeat items may be critical in mapping the spread of a discussion or following a story or event. This may be particularly the case (which we have found in our research) when a press release from an organization prompts a set of news stories which may appear across a range of formal and informal media outlets promoted, shared and commented on across social media. However, in many studies, it is the case that the original online item is the key item of data, but this can be supported by capturing the metadata related to the subsequent flow and sharing that is evident within the broader dataset.
- Identifying and logging the component parts of the data item: online data are often multi-modal and complex in form. These forms will vary depending on the platform and media in use but include a variety of text (including headlines, labels, subheadings, embedded text from other sources) and visual forms (including charts, infographics, photographs, video clips). With regard to each data item, it is also important to decide how to deal with links. These may be embedded or simply listed as related sources. In some studies, these links may be actively pursued as part of the tracking strategy or used as a means to increase the data collected (see above). Alternatively, these may simply be logged as a form of metadata.

As with the earlier discussion of deciding what is included or excluded from the dataset, it is important to document the processes that are adopted in preparing the data for analysis so that there is a clear audit trail. Use research questions as a guide for this process, asking how and to what extent a decision will impact the ability to make a contribution in responding to this question. For example, earlier (Box 2.2) we introduced Jakob's research on paternity leave, in which he posed the following question: To what extent is paternity leave presented as a positive development in media discussions about gender equality? A key issue for Jakob is likely to be to what extent he retains, within the dataset, items that relate primarily to maternity leave, particularly those which perhaps only mention paternity leave in passing. In this case, given Jakob plans to select case studies from his data for in-depth analysis, it does not make sense to retain those articles that contain very little mention of paternity leave. Here Jakob could set a ratio that he feels is appropriate, which might be that he retains the item if at least 1/3 of the content relates to paternity leave. In cases such as this, pragmatic judgement is also critical, particularly when there is a specific deadline and limited resources for the research project. Once again, working with a supervisor or mentor to discuss these **research decisions** will likely prove very helpful.

We would suggest that, using this book as a prompt, it is useful to undertake a preliminary review of the data to identify the specific issues to be resolved before analysis. It may be possible to prepare a small section of data first and then proceed with analysis of these data to review how this decision plays out in the later stages of the research project. As in other forms of qualitative research, reflexivity throughout is key. After all, there is no perfect research project and understanding the limitations of our work is an essential part of the research process.

CHAPTER SUMMARY

In this chapter we have:

- explored practical ways in which a focus can be maintained on a research question as the project proceeds
- reviewed the practical issues associated with conducting a pilot
- considered the ways in which tools and technology can be effectively managed
- provided advice on answering the question: Are these data?
- discussed how to balance the scale of the research undertaking
- outlined the process involved in getting ready for analysis.

Together with the overview provided in the previous chapter, these topics provide guidance on the challenges of tracking and trawling research projects. In the next chapter we go on to review examples of existing research that have successfully published online qualitative research data.

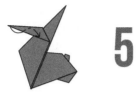

5

EXAMPLES OF COLLECTING QUALITATIVE DATA WITH DIGITAL METHODS

INTRODUCTION

This chapter illustrates the various ways in which qualitative digital data have been collected across published studies in business and management research. Throughout the book we have drawn on our own research practice to illustrate key points relevant to the discussion in hand. We have also presented hypothetical student projects to highlight how different aspects of tracking and trawling might be operationalized. Within this chapter we have deliberately selected a range of studies that have explored different topics within the management field, engaged with diverse forms of online data and adopted a variety of strategies within their research projects.

As engagement with online qualitative data is still an emergent area of research in our field, this is reflected in the status of the methodological accounts within the papers we have reviewed (both here and more broadly). To date research has lacked an established repository of practice and there have been few methodological guides that focus on data collection. Research practices are therefore widely varied and often creatively adaptive to the challenges faced. Given this, we suggest it is important for you to read widely across a range of existing research rather than 'cherry pick' a particular approach from a single paper. Indeed, our review has further found that accounts provided in published papers rarely provide sufficient detail to act as a guide for others. This observation is not intended as a criticism of these authors. Rather it is a common challenge of publishing qualitative research in reputable journals that word count restrictions often lead to summarized methodological accounts, and within these more attention is usually given to data analysis rather than collection. Taking Höllerer et al. (2013) as a case, this account describes how 37 reports from 12 different organizations were collected and analysed in relation to images of corporate social responsibility. These reports could have been obtained by a number of means but, as an appendix provides the URL for each report, we might assume that they were downloaded from the Internet as a result of an online search process.

Relatedly, we observe that the temporality of data collection is often described in very broad terms and therefore it is sometimes difficult to determine whether researchers have looked back over a previous period (via trawling) or collected data in real-time for the specified days, weeks or months (via tracking). Of course, this is a particular feature that we highlight as significant for understandings of tracking and trawling (see Chapter 1) as set out across this book. Although, as we acknowledge, while this differentiation is methodologically useful, the application of methods in practice often combines these aspects in various ways, as will be seen in the examples reviewed across this chapter.

Above we highlighted that because this is a relatively new area of research, studies are often adapting to research challenges in real time. Unsurprisingly a range of responses are in evidence in the studies we have reviewed. In particular, accounts focus on the challenge of managing large quantities of data, either expected or experienced. In some studies, we see relatively small timeframes specified within which data are collected. The assumption here is that limiting the duration of data collection will help contain the volume of data collected. It is also the case that with the dynamic and transitory nature of Internet material (see also Chapter 1) having a restricted timeframe makes it easier to 'fix' the dataset. However, the rationale for the timeframe is often left unclear. Specifying how dates were selected and particularly if they relate to events relevant to the research topics can help readers understand why and how the timeframe is pertinent to the research undertaking. We found that researchers also used other criteria such as organizational type as a means of managing the scale of data collection. In these cases, the criteria are usually more clearly specified and contextualized in relation to the research scope.

Elsewhere, we see more extensive data collection periods, and often much larger datasets as a result. Here, as in some of the examples below, we see a subsequent process of refining the dataset during the transition to analysis to manage the quantity of data. Perhaps understandably, quantitative criteria are often deployed in this process. In contrast in our own research (Whiting and Pritchard, 2020) we have explained how we used the notion of a **discursive event** as a means of extracting a smaller dataset for interrogation from a much longer (150 days in our case) research project. A discursive event can be viewed as a **bounded episode** (Hardy and Maguire, 2010) related to a significant occurrence around which data collection might be focused, or in our case extracted from a larger dataset. We used the publication of a particular report related to retirement as the event under consideration (Whiting and Pritchard, 2020).

A further point of note in considering the examples explored below is the various ways in which researchers have dealt with ethical issues in research. Again, these are not always fully explicated within published papers. Sometimes online data collection is positioned as secondary data (Ozdora-Aksak and Atakan-Duman, 2015) and in other examples the researchers state that their institutions regard data in the public domain as outside the scope of ethical review (Kelly et al., 2012). Similar diversity is encountered in how researchers relate to copyright issues, particularly regarding the reproduction of images within research publications.

Using the framework we have established across previous chapters, we first explore those studies that are most closely aligned with tracking approaches before moving on to consider trawling studies. We acknowledge that the inclusion under one or other heading within this chapter is based on our reading of the author's description of research methods and these are not terms or classifications used within the studies themselves. Indeed, in light of the discussion above the grouping of studies is not a straightforward endeavour, particularly as tracking and trawling are not discrete terms but rather represent a spectrum of approaches. We then explore studies that employ data collection methods that run across this spectrum before looking at research which has combined tracking and trawling with other data collection approaches, usually those involving direct interaction with participants. Throughout we have selected examples that together cover a wider range of qualitative Internet data types and in particular highlight the authors' views on challenges encountered during their research endeavours.

The following topics are explored in this chapter:

- tracking studies
- trawling studies
- tracking and trawling combined
- tracking and trawling combined with additional data collection methods.

TRACKING STUDIES

In this section we offer examples of research that has applied tracking approaches across a range of topics and online contexts. As a topic, corporate social responsibility (CSR) has been the subject of particular scrutiny for those using digital methods to collect qualitative Internet data. This stems from the popularity of this and closely related topics (such as global warming and wealth disparity) across online media. Ozdora-Aksak and Atakan-Duman (2015) undertook a study of the ways in which Turkish banks present corporate social responsibility activities to support and enhance their broader organizational identity. In this study, the researchers tracked the eight largest Turkish banks (by size of branch network) over a four-month period and downloaded data from both corporate websites and social media, describing this as secondary data. Specifically, they downloaded text from the informational sections of the banks' websites: 'about us, history, mission and vision, and corporate social responsibility sections' (Ozdora-Aksak and Atakan-Duman, 2015: 122). However, while they were able to identify common sections across the banks' corporate websites from which to download data, the authors found the social media data more challenging. This was because at the time of the study the use of social media varied hugely across the eight banks selected in the study. However, they collected both text and images from Twitter and Facebook over a four-month period, which resulted in data ranging from 39 items for one bank to 429 for another; both quantitative and qualitative methods were then used for analysis. Ozdora-Aksak and Atakan-Duman (2015) report that their analysis showed differences between categories of banks and types of online data, stating that the volume of material collected in relation to CSR was itself informative.

Continuing on a theme related to CSR, Kassinis and Panayiotou (2017) conducted a tracking study that focused on a single organization, BP. Their focus was to explore the issue of corporate hypocrisy in relation to stated CSR objectives. This study was conducted over five years and involved bi-weekly downloads of webpages. One issue the authors highlight was the challenge of maintaining a consistent approach to data collection over a long period of time during which the website underwent many changes. Kassinis and Panayiotou (2017) highlighted how they focused on the organization's home page, monitoring changes on a bi-weekly basis. They also note that their research focus changed, particularly since the Deepwater Horizon oil rig accident occurred during their study. While this is beyond the timeframe for a Masters research project, their account highlights that there may be considerable periods of inactivity, but in the wake of the Deepwater Horizon incident they increased to a system of daily monitoring for a period of six months. This allowed them to refocus the research and make use of a before-during-after account of CSR.

Adopting a similar focus on a single entity, but on a different scale and topic, Swan's (2017) research focuses on an individual entrepreneur's website and offers an in-depth multi-modal analysis of 'postfeminist stylistics' (2017: 286). This was originally part of a broader study that was tracking 20 websites related to coaching for women. Indeed, these sites had themselves been identified as part of a broader trawling-type study on this topic over a ten-month period. As highlighted previously, this reflects the often interrelated nature of tracking and trawling studies and how one may emerge as a focus in later stages of data collection. In this paper, Swan specifically focuses on the website of an individual coach and entrepreneur, downloading all the webpages using a screenshot tool over a ten-month period. She highlights that this website was selected because it was 'visually striking and hence conducive to a visual analysis, and exemplified a number of themes' related to her research focus (Swan, 2017: 280). Swan specifically discusses the ethical issues of her research. She notes the difference between the online persona and the 'real' offline person and focuses her analytic attention on the online 'imagined coach' (2017: 282). However, given the explicit focus on an individual, Swan sought and obtained ethical consent from the individual concerned. This is unusual in Internet research of this type. Swan's research highlighted the different ways in which the text, visuals and layout of the webpages acted to confirm and recirculate key understandings central to postfeminism with a focus on supporting different forms of 'feminine labour – emotional work, self-work, caring work and digital labour' (2017: 292).

Moving to a different area of research, there has been particular interest in the way in which recruitment practices have evolved alongside the development of the Internet. Boland's (2016) study aimed to investigate the ways in which the identity of 'jobseeker' is constructed online. His research used Google search results rankings to identify those websites that were most likely to be encountered by unemployed jobseekers in the UK. This included government sites and recruitment agencies. While there is little detail on the specific techniques involved, Boland reports downloading over 100 pages of advice from the six most popular websites, citing saturation as a rationale for regarding this was a comprehensive dataset. Boland notes in particular the way the notion of enterprise and self-advancement is central to the advice provided to jobseekers, with limited use of support frameworks. It is useful to note that saturation is a common rationale used within qualitative research, which here was identified in the repetitive nature of the data downloaded. This argument requires careful consideration as the nature and value of saturation is highly debated (Saunders et al., 2018). However, particularly within Masters research projects, we acknowledge that it provides a further useful means of managing the quantity of data to take forward to data analysis.

Glozer et al.'s (2019) study investigated the ways in which organizations interact on social media sites and the ways in which these lead to legitimizing accounts of organizational action and interest. The case focused on two food retailers with discussions on topics ranging from plastic use to gender taking place on the organizations' main public Facebook pages. This study focused on Facebook, with the authors engaging in an initial period of online observation, which takes this close to some descriptions of netnography (Kozinets et al., 2014). Subsequently, the Facebook pages of these two organizations were tracked over a period of 11 months. An initial broad set of **discussion threads** was identified but these threads were then reviewed to focus on four discussion topics that occurred across the different sites. The authors then described how they traced within these sites to track back to the origins of the selected discussions so that these data could also be analysed. The authors conceptualize these discussion threads as **polyphonic** data that emerge in interaction between organizational members and public visitors to the Facebook pages of these companies. Glozer et al. (2019) provide a particularly useful account of the steps taken with regard to research ethics. In particular, while the raw data were analysed, and shared with reviewers, they cloaked data extracts in the publication to ensure anonymity of those contributors. The research highlights the importance of micro-discourse within social media as a means of exploring how ideas become legitimated.

Focusing on a different topic, data type and platform, Rokka and Canniford (2016) were also interested in the interaction between organizational and consumer narratives, here in relation to champagne consumption. This study tracked both organizational and consumer generated images on Instagram, following three well-known brands of champagne and using a tool called Brandwatch to support data collection. The authors captured data across a six-week period in 2014, which resulted in a dataset of over 6,000 consumer and nearly 2,000 brand images. Given this volume, 100 images of each type were then randomly selected for initial analysis with the number further reduced for later detailed analysis. Adopting a version of the cloaking that Glozer et al. (2019) describe, here the authors had 'an artist render photographic images as accurate illustrations, so as to preserve the integrity of images in a manner that avoids copyright or privacy violations' (Rokka and Canniford, 2016: 1804). Interestingly when we approached our own individual institutions regarding adopting a similar approach for a visual research project, we received mixed advice on this as a solution to the challenge of using images in journal publications. As we review further below (Boje and Smith, 2010) this remains a particularly challenging issue for researchers. However, studies such as Rokka and Canniford's (2016) highlight the importance of new visual forms such as the selfie in digital research.

Our own research on age used a tracking approach to collect qualitative online data. In our study on generational identities (Pritchard and Whiting, 2014) we used data identified from Google Alerts over 150 days but also generated additional data via snowballing from links these alerts provided and by downloading below-the-line comments, where these were available. This search protocol was developed after pilot testing, discussed earlier in Chapters 3 and 4 (Pritchard and Whiting, 2012a). All our data came from public sources that did not require any form of log-in to access. Across our broader research project, we collected over 1,000 sources, and noted that 'a source might include multiple texts as both articles and posted comments were saved together. Sources range from the equivalent of one paragraph to over sixty pages of text' (Pritchard and Whiting, 2014: 1611). In our paper on generations we extracted the data associated with two generational identities (the lost generation and baby boomers) as found within UK online news sources. The resulting data comprised texts totaling 24,000 words for baby boomers and 25,000 words related to the lost generation. In contrast to Glozer et al. (2019), we did not deploy any form of cloaking in publishing our data (Pritchard and Whiting, 2014), as we felt that amendments might change meanings and could inadvertently identify an alternative source for the text. Within our broader project, we have also collected images, but our approach here has encompassed other data collection methods and is discussed later in the chapter.

All the studies reviewed in this section applied innovative approaches to collecting (and indeed the subsequent analysing of) qualitative Internet data. In general, however, this research falls towards the tracking end of the spectrum, so we move on to consider trawling studies below.

TRAWLING STUDIES

The first study we review in this section undertook a trawling approach within a specific social media context: YouTube. Kelly et al.'s (2012) study investigated the ways in which nurses' identities were constructed in YouTube clips. Using 'nurse' and 'nursing' as search terms (and undertaking a subsequent review to delete clips related to breastfeeding) the authors trawled YouTube clips posted between 2005 and 2010. This search took place over a two-day period and identified nearly 300,000 clips. To contain the data collection process the authors focused on the top 50 links for each search term, storing links within an Excel spreadsheet, copying clip informaton for YouTube and noting the number of views. Subsequently they offer a detailed analysis of the ten most popular clips within their analysis, reflecting later that popularity is only one possible measure of influence.

Interestingly, the authors also report on their discussions regarding ethical approval within their institutions, noting they were advised that 'our reporting of results of our discourse analysis had no ethical import for individuals portrayed in the video clips, and accordingly, the study was not subjected to ethical review' (Kelly et al., 2012: 1806).

Indeed, many visual studies have used trawling approaches to identify images for analysis. One useful example of this approach is Delmestri et al. (2015) who downloaded the emblems and logos of 821 universities in a study of web-branding. The authors state that they visited the front pages of all universities in 19 countries and a sample from America, using the online source Braintrack to identify institutions and their websites. From this they 'compiled a database of the icons used by each university for self-representation in the front page of the Internet home page' (Delmestri et al., 2015: 125). Applying content analysis, the authors explored international differences in representation.

Looking at a different topic entirely, Duffy and Hund (2015) explored the self-representation of female entrepreneurs. This research identified the top 38 US fashion blogs based on the ranking on the site Bloglovin. They highlight that their interest in self-presentation led to a decision to only focus on bloggers who had less than ten employees and ensured that the bloggers were still active and not syndicated by a larger media company. While the details of the collection process are not provided, the authors explain that they focused on the 'about me' section of a blog, substituting a search for a media interview if this was not available. In addition they collected a further 760 Instagram images, collecting 20 images from accounts linked to each blog. Their in-depth qualitative analysis of both texts and images relates to notions of 'having it all' and the challenges of maintaining this self-presentation.

Other trawling studies have deployed search protocols within specific social media sites or platforms to identify data of relevance. Returning to textual data, van Bommel and Spicer's (2011) study of Slow Food focused on journalistic reporting of this trend, and the authors acknowledge that they took some time to conduct background research before commencing data collection. They were interested in examining representation in media texts within the UK, noting the importance of media in re-presenting the movement to members and broader audiences, not least since the founder was a journalist. The authors focused on broadsheet newspapers in the UK (see also Box 2.2) and accessed these as qualitative Internet data via an online ser- vice provider (here, Factiva). They used a ten-year search period and the term 'slow food', resulting in a sample of 142 news articles for analysis. The authors undertook a chronological discourse analysis reviewing the changing arguments used to enrol readers in support of the Slow Food movement.

Moor and Kanji (2019) used the advanced search facility within the Mumsnet forum for a research project focused on money and relationships. Searching over a four- month period they identified 36 relevant discussion threads, ranging from 13 to 681 messages within the thread structures, reviewing the ways in which interactions pro- vide support for particular negotiation approaches. In their paper, the authors review the public nature of Mumsnet discussions, explaining their view that its use does not necessarily require consent from individuals' (Moor and Kanji, 2019: 8). However, some researchers have explicitly requested permission from Mumsnet for research access (Hine, 2014) and while this is cited as a protocol, it is not clear whether these researchers followed this process. The specifics of any research project should always be discussed with the relevant institutional representatives for ethics to ensure the appropriate processes are followed.

Reddit is another social media site that has received particular research attention, again because of the public nature of the discussion boards, which provides reassur- ance when considering issues of research ethics. Chang-Kredl and Colannino (2017) explored the construction of teacher identity using Reddit data obtained after key word searches (such as best teacher, worst teacher). They trawled Reddit discussion threads from 2009 to 2015 and selected the data for analysis in two phases. The first phase involved selecting those threads with the highest number of posts (as an indication of popularity). This resulted in a dataset that contained eight threads - four each related to positive ('best teacher') and negative ('worst teacher') constructions of identity. From eight threads a further process of data selection was undertaken, which involved reading all posts to identify those posts that related to an individual's memory of a teacher. Next the most popular within each thread were selected, with a maximum of 100 posts taken from each thread. This resulted in 600 posts/comments in the final dataset. The authors (Chang-Kredl and Colannino, 2017) explain that they used the principle of saturation as a means of deciding when sufficient data had been identified (O'Reilly and Parker, 2013).

In another study trawling Reddit for data, Lillqvist et al. (2018) used posts on Reddit to examine the interaction between marketers and consumers and how these act to legitimize marketing constructs. In their methods description the authors usefully break down the different types of posts on Reddit distinguishing between sponsored posts, a type of post known as 'ask me anything', posts with relevant links, specific marketing discussions and also posts related to Reddit rules. Indeed, they break down different characteristics of post types within their analysis to consider how characteristics are related to content. This was particularly relevant to the focus of their study, the interaction between marketers and consumers. They go on to explain that the process by which data were selected via trawling involved a process of 'close reading' (Lillqvist et al., 2018: 191) to select extracts for analysis.

Pearce et al. (2018) highlight that many of the studies undertaken with online qualitative data have drawn from either one or a limited number of sites or platforms. Indeed, this focus is often highlighted as a means of managing dataset size. The authors note, as we have earlier in our book, that researchers need to be aware of the implications of, and reflect fully on, platform choice in their projects. Pearce et al. (2018) outline a process named visual cross-platform analysis (VCPA), which involves collecting data from multiple platforms. In the example presented (regarding images of climate change) data are drawn from Instagram, Facebook, Twitter, Reddit and **Tumblr**, with a resulting set of nearly 500,000 images identified for analysis. Reflecting the multi-platform nature of this data, a number of tools were used to collect data although the process for trawling is not unpacked. It is important to note that this scale of research project is likely to be well beyond the scope of most Masters research projects, hence we do not fully explore the method in detail. However, it serves to highlight the importance of examining assumptions about platforms and data.

TRACKING AND TRAWLING COMBINED

As outlined at the start of this chapter, categorizing existing research along the spectrum of tracking and trawling is not always straightforward. In the examples above, it is possible to see some aspects of tracking within a trawling study and vice versa. Here we explore studies where the combination is more explicitly recognized within the methodological accounts.

Boje and Smith (2010) studied understandings of the successful entrepreneur using case studies of both Virgin (Richard Branson) and Microsoft (Bill Gates). This involved a process of tracking these two corporate websites for both textual and visual data in addition to trawling the Internet for what they term 'unauthorized' images, namely cartoons and caricatures. This research involved both directed tracking within the boundaries of the websites but also a broader trawling approach to identify other depictions of Bill Gates and Richard Branson to contrast and compare with these constructions. The research involves a step-by-step review of each website together with an analysis of cartoons. The authors also usefully reflect on the challenges of using web images which, both ethically and with regards to copyright legislation, seem to fall 'in a contested "no man's land" (2010: 315) with regards the right to reproduce within journal publications. This challenge may account for why many studies of visual images do not include the images themselves within published accounts.

Sundstrom and Levenshus's (2017) study of how media companies engage via Twitter provides a useful example of a study that both tracks and trawls on this platform. This research aimed to understand the approaches organizations deploy to gain engagement via Twitter, within the context of understanding effective public relations strategies. Twitter is a particularly flexible platform for this research approach because of the way tweets can be both accessed historically and followed forwards. The authors used financial data to identify 25 potential media companies for their study. These were then tracked on Twitter for a week to see if they were active (defined as at least one tweet in that week). This reduced the sample to 18 media companies. From these company Twitter accounts, the authors then trawled 'the most recent 100 tweets collected in reverse chronological order' (2017: 22). The data collected included the tweet content but also the related threads along with interaction data. Using content analysis, this research then explored the different tactics used by these media companies including the ways in which they acted as both content originators and content distributors.

As explored in Chapter 1, our own research has also frequently involved a combination of tracking and trawling. For our paper on reconstructing retirement (Whiting and Pritchard, 2020) we utilized both data that we had obtained through tracking (via Google Alerts) and trawling. In this case trawling used both a snowballing technique following links in data we had identified during our tracking and a targeted key term search focused on a particular phrase of relevance to our research question. This enabled us to identify a full range of data related to a particular publication on the future of retirement for older workers.

With the scope of a Masters research project, tracking and trawling can be effectively combined; however, it is important to ensure that the scope of this activity is managed and that such combination is essential to the research question studied.

TRACKING AND TRAWLING COMBINED WITH ADDITIONAL DATA COLLECTION METHODS

It is becoming increasingly popular to utilize qualitative Internet data at part of a broader multi-method study. As with the caveat above regarding combining tracking and trawling, this can be useful for a Masters research project providing the scope is well managed. This might involve using a small focused trawling process to identify topic relevant social media data, which can then be used as prompts for discussion within an interview schedule. Adopting a slightly different approach in our research on age at work, we have used online images that were collected during a tracking study within a group photo-elicitation activity, while also undertaking our own **visual analysis** of these images (Pritchard and Whiting, 2015, 2017). In our data collection, we originally identified 120 usable images. This was far smaller than the total number available, as we excluded images where there was insufficient copyright information, photographs of named individuals and poor quality reproductions. In focusing on a specific research question (related to representations of gendered ageing) we then decided to concentrate our analysis on stock images and further narrowed our data to those photographs that we coded as related to gendered ageing. This resulted in a dataset of 16 photographs. From further analysis using Rose (2012) and Davison (2010) we identified a sub-set of three photographs to use in a group photo-elicitation workshop that involved 39 participants in total. Our report of this study includes both our own visual analysis of these images along with a thematic analysis of participants' responses to the images displayed. In sum, we found that the subject positioning in respect of gendered ageing can be problematic for both men and women though in different ways and at different ages.

Orlikowski and Scott's (2014) study showed how data from social media platforms can be integrated within a broader qualitative research project. Here the platforms were TripAdvisor and the AA hotel review website. The authors combined tracking 16 hotels across these sites with visits and a broad interview programme to examine the impact of online reviews with those involved. They also undertook some trawling for media coverage of online reviews. This was an extensive and comprehensive study that goes well beyond the scope of the typical Masters research project but highlights how specific platforms can be used with related research questions. Situated in relation to evaluation practices, this research 'explains both how valuations are actively produced in ongoing practice and how their production is significantly reconfiguring everyday practices of the organizations being evaluated' (2014: 868).

A further study that uses a range of different sources is Bell and Leonard's (2018) review of digital organizational storytelling. This focuses on one case organization (a media company) and involved a mix of multi-modal data including YouTube videos, documents and interviews. During this research project, the authors watched all of the case organization's YouTube videos and reviewed comments posted by other viewers as well as tracking Facebook, Twitter and other corporate sites and conducted seven interviews. The authors discuss how their research offers insights into the form and function of digital organizational storytelling, and in particular how they 'identified the network protocols of affinity, authenticity and amateurism that frame how a story is understood, and whether or not it is deemed plausible' (Bell and Leonard, 2018: 348). In another innovative study, Baxter and Marcella (2017) explored how voters accessed information during the Scottish referendum and conducted interviews during which participants were asked to undertake a search for information online using handheld devices. They called this an 'interactive, electronically-assisted interview method' (Baxter and Marcella, 2017: 540) during which the participants are effectively undertaking the trawling activity themselves. In analysing the data collected, the authors reviewed the different characteristics of media that influence voter intention. These studies show the innovative ways that tracking and trawling can be used with other qualitative methods across a range of areas of investigation.

CHAPTER SUMMARY

In this chapter we have:

- discussed the challenges of identifying existing research that utilizes a tracking and/or trawling approach
- highlighted existing research across a variety of topics and platforms that have collected qualitative Internet data using online methods
- explored the different approaches and issues highlighted in published research that has undertaken tracking and/or trawling activities
- examined research projects that have utilized tracking and trawling in combination and in combination with other methods of data collection.

The studies explored here illustrate the breadth of research that can be undertaken with tracking and trawling approaches. However, they do not offer recipes that can simply be applied to a Masters research project and are used here for illustrative purposes. When considering a new research project, it is important to consult widely regarding potential methodological approaches, including other reviews of online research (Pearce et al., 2018; Snelson, 2016).

6

CONCLUSIONS

INTRODUCTION

In this chapter, we critique tracking and trawling as a qualitative digital data collection method by setting out their advantages and disadvantages and considering what makes a good qualitative Internet data collection method. We then outline the next steps in the research process by anticipating data analysis and the writing up of the findings. We conclude with a summary of what this book has covered and provide suggestions for further readings.

CRITIQUING TRACKING AND TRAWLING

The preceding chapters have covered all the stages involved in qualitative Internet data collection using tracking and trawling. We critique these methods by outlining the advantages and disadvantages for the Masters research student of tracking and trawling as a means of qualitative digital data collection.

Advantages of tracking and trawling

We outlined at the start of this book how the Internet presents considerable opportunities for researchers at every stage in their careers. For those tackling their Masters research dissertations, the decision to use digital methods of qualitative Internet data collection represents an opportunity to engage with some of the latest communication technologies in pursuit of examining our 'most comprehensive electronic archive' (Eysenbach and Till, 2001: 1103). Doing so has several advantages. First, tracking and trawling can be very quick and efficient ways to collect a substantial volume of data. For tracking, once the tools have been set up, piloted and adjusted as necessary, some forms of alerts will generate links without further handling (though obviously the researcher will need to be involved in assessing the material linked to for relevance and uploading). For trawling, with its focus on identifying material that has already been posted on the Internet, this can be a very fast way to collect data. The methods also allow for the preparation, management and analysis of collected data before all data collection is completed, a characteristic shared with some other methods of qualitative data collection such as interviews (Cassell, 2015). This enables a certain efficiency (analysing early data while later data are still being collated), which can save time overall. This relative speed and flexibility are useful for the Masters research student who will have limited time in which to design, carry out and write up a research project.

The second advantage is that these methods utilize skills that the researcher may already have acquired in the course of everyday activities involving the Internet. While we reiterate the point from Chapter 1 that tracking and trawling are distinct from regular web browsing, most researchers will have a familiarity with the Internet and its interfaces, which may ease the transition to using digital data collection methods in contrast to other methods of data collection such as interviews or surveys where the researcher may not have any comparable transferable experience. Third, tracking and trawling do not require the recruitment of participants, which can be time-consuming to arrange and where the researcher may encounter barriers to participation, for example, in the course of negotiating access via organizational gatekeepers. Fourth, the methods are very flexible and can be adapted to suit many different topics and research questions; they are also compatible with a range of epistemological positions. Finally, the methods are responsive and adaptive so that they can be adjusted during the data collection period in response to new material that the researcher uncovers (conceptual or empirical) and to new ideas. They can also be used in combination with other methods (for example, to collect data that can be used as heuristic prompts in interviews or to supplement a methodology where the amount of expected data has fallen short of expectations).

Disadvantages of tracking and trawling

There are limitations to any data collection method. For tracking and trawling, the first and key disadvantage is that the relative ease with which large volumes of potential data present themselves to the researcher is a rather daunting prospect. It is relatively easy to set up alerts or trawl the Internet for material, but it can be difficult to scope the boundaries of data collection to make it manageable and focused. Good piloting can help with this. So does maintaining focus: as we highlighted in Chapter 4, the researcher will need to keep asking themselves whether the material being identified actually addresses the research question(s). Developing a list of criteria for assessing relevance is very useful.

Second, a related issue is that data handling and management can be time-consuming. In addition to reviewing for relevance, the actual checking of links to Internet material, and uploading relevant data into the researcher's chosen data management system takes time. We created a step by step protocol for data handling in our pilot study, which was very helpful as we progressed through a total of 150 days of data collection (Pritchard and Whiting, 2012a). We did this because with two of us involved we needed transparency between ourselves but actually a protocol is useful for the researcher working on their own (not least when writing up the method). We found that regular (at least every second day) reviewing of the daily alerts (from tracking) and potential material (from trawling) helped keep on top of the process. In the end, it provided us with an overall dataset that was within manageable proportions and crucially within the timescale required by our funded project.

This leads us to the third disadvantage, namely that Internet-based data are not durable and may disappear without warning. This underlines the need for handling the data promptly; downloading it and uploading it in a stable permanent form is critical for it to be available for later analysis. The fourth disadvantage is that Internet research relies on using proprietary tools, which are subject to their own limitations in terms of what they can and cannot do. The researcher must check these carefully when selecting the tool, or combination of tools, and take care not to over-interpret the findings but to position them within the boundaries of the data collection enabled by the tools. For instance, the Twitter search application program interface (API) only provides 1 per cent of actual traffic (Burnap et al., 2015). The fifth disadvantage is that the volume of data can be unpredictable. If faced with large volumes of relevant material, then the issues already addressed in this section can help. However, there is the possibility that, despite a promising pilot study, the methods do not generate either the volume or quality of data expected. If the researcher is reviewing the links regularly, they will be able to spot this early and make adjustments. This might include revising alerts for tracking, conducting more trawling for relevant material already posted or could include combining these methods with another data collection method such as interviews (for example, with individuals identified in the tracking and trawling data). The final disadvantage is that the ethical considerations of qualitative Internet research can be complex. Although there is more detailed guidance now available, it can take time to work through this in relation to a project and the researcher may encounter delays in the process of seeking ethical approval if their institution is not familiar with this area.

Overall, however, we recommend tracking and trawling as methods of qualitative Internet data collection. They are distinct from methods such as netnography (Kozinets, 2019; Kozinets et al., 2014) as discussed in Chapter 5, so that they represent additional methodological tools for the qualitative researcher. Their adaptability and flexibility in being able to address many research topics across a range of philosophical approaches, as well as the opportunity to craft a dataset relatively quickly, make them invaluable for the Masters research project student. As we have said earlier, no research project will be perfect or free of issues, the key is to be prepared. Being reflexive is a helpful starting point as we discuss next in our consideration of what makes for good data collection.

WHAT MAKES A GOOD QUALITATIVE INTERNET DATA COLLECTION METHOD?

The issue of assessing what constitutes good qualitative research is not straightforward. It is also argued that 'having one agreed set of criteria may threaten to undermine the very characteristics of qualitative research that are valued by the research community' (Symon et al., 2018: 144). This might be confusing for the novice researcher wondering if the data collection for their project is 'good enough'.

One reason that the criteria for assessing qualitative research are somewhat contested (Cassell and Symon, 2011; Symon et al., 2018) is the variety of different philosophical traditions on which qualitative research can be based. This is particularly the case in Europe (more so than in the US) and the use of these philosophies has helped to make visible and acceptable alternatives to positivist quantitative approaches (Symon and Cassell, 2016). These approaches – such as the 'big data' movement that dominates much Internet research (Dutton, 2013) – are synonymous with the criteria of validity and reliability. However, it is important to remember that these were developed to address very specific issues in relation to quantitative methods used within the positivist tradition deploying statistical analyses (Symon et al., 2018). Many argue that it is not appropriate or indeed possible to assess qualitative research by these criteria (for example, Easterby-Smith et al., 2008). What criteria should be used instead? Symon and colleagues (2018) argue that what constitutes appropriate criteria depends on context and culture. They call for a more pluralistic approach that involves a reflexive evaluation of research, one that recognizes that empirical studies can be grounded in a wide range of different philosophic traditions.

We argue that a good data collection method is one which is performed ethically, is carried out commensurate with its philosophical assumptions (its ontology and epistemology that we discussed in Chapter 2) and results in high-quality data that addresses the research question(s). We also maintain that one of the key strengths of qualitative research (done well) is the contribution afforded by reflexivity. In the context of assessing quality, demonstrating validity is often said to be relevant. In qualitative research, this might involve constructing a narrative 'to explain ... what was done and why' in order to demonstrate 'why and how the [research] findings are legitimate' (Phillips and Hardy, 2002: 79). As Mason concludes, the best way to demonstrate validity is to 'explain how you came to the conclusion that your methods were valid' (2002: 190). This brings us to the point made in Chapters 3 and 4 about the need for ongoing reflexivity and how this needs to be actively managed to ensure that the focus and relevance of the research question is maintained. Each stage of the tracking and trawling methods, such as an effective pilot study, provides the researcher with an opportunity for reflexivity around their own decision-making and more generally about the research process. If the researcher has created an audit trail by making comprehensive notes of what they have done and why certain choices have been made, this will be invaluable in writing up the methods chapter of a Masters research dissertation and can usefully inform the discussion section too. This level of reflexive detail also enables a full consideration and critique of the methodology and its validity. This is an essential step in conducting and demonstrating a good data collection method.

AFTER THE DATA COLLECTION: NEXT STEPS

Once the researcher has finished data collection, they will need to prepare for analysing the data and writing up their dissertation. We look at what is involved in these next stages in the project.

Preparing for data analysis

We have partly anticipated preparation for data analysis in our discussion of data management in Chapters 3 and 4. This is a point of difference perhaps with other qualitative data collection methods; for tracking and trawling the management of data is less distinct from its collection. This may be due to the need to convert material from the Internet into something that is stable and permanent whereas, in other methods, data are usually created in a form which already complies with this requirement. It is therefore likely that by this stage the researcher using tracking and trawling has already made the decision whether to use CAQDAS or not. As well as enabling data management, these software packages can be used to organize data and support analysis, though it is important to remember that it is the researcher and not the software who actually does the analysing and interpreting.

Having a data management system in place is, however, only the starting point. As well as the data being in a form that can be interrogated, the researcher needs to have a strategy for doing the interrogation. A possible complexity is if the data are in different forms, including potentially a mix of both textual and visual. These may require different analytic treatments. In terms of selecting a method of data analysis, a key starting point is to reflect on the philosophical underpinnings of the research and to select a method that fits. Some analytic techniques like template analysis are flexible and can be used with a variety of ontological and epistemological assumptions. Others such as discourse analysis are consistent with a particular (specifically social constructionist) epistemology. Some are really only suited to images such as visual frame analysis (Fahmy et al., 2007) or Davison's (2010) visual portraiture codes. Others such as content analysis are primarily designed for analysing text (for example, Ozdora-Aksak and Atakan-Duman, 2015) but can be adapted to visual data (Rokka and Canniford, 2016).

A detailed discussion of the various methods of data analysis that could be used with qualitative textual and visual Internet data is outside the scope of this book. Other volumes in this series address these in detail. In Chapter 5, as part of our review of examples of research using tracking and trawling methods, we include studies where different analytic methods have been used, which we believe will be helpful for researchers as they tackle this next stage in their project.

Initial tips for data analysis

As we have discussed in the advantages of tracking and trawling, these methods enable the researcher to start analysing their data before all of it is collected. This is useful given that qualitative analysis methods are quite time-consuming, and the time-bound dissertation researcher is well advised to start analysis as soon as possible as otherwise the task can easily become daunting and unmanageable. In interviews the researcher is present as the data are collected, indeed, we would say that the interview data are co-constructed by participant and researcher. When a researcher receives or creates the transcripts of an interview, they will have some familiarity with the content from having been present at its creation. This is different in tracking and trawling. The researcher is very much part of the construction of the data, deciding the topic focus, the parameters of search terms and other key aspects of the research design. But we argue that the content of the material that is made available to the researcher as potential data as a result of these methods will be unexpected. Assessing for relevance will usually be quite a quick process so often the first full read through of, say, a news article or blog post will be the first time that the researcher comes face to face with their data. And this - which is familiarization - is the first step in data analysis.

In Table 6.1 we set out examples of different methods of data analysis that have been used in published studies involving qualitative Internet data. We have also organized these by reference to the underlying philosophical assumptions of the research to give an indication of paradigm commensurability with regard to the analytic method.

Table 6.1 Examples of analytic methods used with textual and visual Internet data in published studies

Philosophical approach	Analytic methods used with textual Internet data (with examples of published study)	Analytic methods used with visual Internet data (with examples of published study)
Qualitative post-positivism	Qualitative content analysis of Twitter profiles and tweets from 18 of the world's largest media companies (Sundstrom and Levenshus, 2017) Quantitative content analysis of 275 randomly sampled legally incorporated non-profit organizations' Facebook profiles (Waters et al., 2009)	Visual content analysis of icons used by universities for self-representation on Internet front pages (Delmestri et al., 2015)
Interpretivist	Thematic content analysis of the corporate websites and social media accounts (Facebook and Twitter) of the eight largest banks in Turkey (Ozdora-Aksak and Atakan-Duman, 2015) Foucauldian discourse analysis of six popular websites that include job advertisements and job-seeking advice (Boland, 2016)	Visual analysis of stock photos of men and women of various ages in relation to work in UK online news (Pritchard and Whiting, 2015)
Critical approaches	Discourse analysis of public Facebook sites of two contrasting food retailing organizations (Glozer et al., 2019) Content analysis combined with discourse analysis of texts found on 24 websites of 10 different companies (Mescher et al., 2010)	Visual content analysis of three popular champagne brand accounts and consumer-made selfies featuring these brands on Instagram (Rokka and Canniford, 2016) Visual narrative analysis and semiotic analysis of the corporate website of BP (Kassinis and Panayiotou, 2017)

CONCLUSIONS

In this book we have introduced tracking and trawling and addressed the underlying philosophical assumptions that inform the uses of these methods. We have covered the core steps that a Masters research student will need to undertake in collecting qualitative Internet data, identified their key components and considered how these may be organized to use the methods. We have provided examples of published studies that have used the methods. The book has concluded by reflecting on the strengths and weaknesses of tracking and trawling, some tips on preparing for data analysis and suggestions for further reading.

Qualitative researchers face a challenge from the prominence of quantitative methods where notions of 'big data' are becoming increasingly synonymous with Internet research (Dutton, 2013). We think that qualitative approaches have much to offer in generating more in-depth understandings of human/digital interactions and examining experiences shaped through and by the Internet. However, we have more methodological work to do to secure a voice for such 'small data' qualitative approaches in a rapidly evolving 'big data' world. A great starting point is for the next generation of researchers, those currently doing their Masters research projects, to engage with qualitative Internet data collection.

GLOSSARY

Achievability   A service provider for higher education in the area of Survey Data Analytics whose aim is to help higher education institutions gain insights into teaching and develop learning structure.

Alternative perspectives   Approaches to topics that challenge traditional or mainstream thinking in a particular area, for example, through examining how campaign groups frame the topic in ways that might call for changes in prevalent conceptualizations, practices and structures.

Application Programming Interface (API)   A set of routines, communication protocols and tools for building software applications, which specifies how software components should interact. This interface between a client and a server is intended to simplify the building of client-side software. There are many different types of APIs for operating systems, applications or websites.

AQUAD   Open-source freeware that supports analysis of various kinds of qualitative data: texts, audio-data such as interview recordings, video data and pictures such as photos or drawings.

Association of Internet Researchers (AoIR)   An international academic association set up to advance the cross-disciplinary field of Internet studies. It is a member-based support network that aims to promote, for example, through its annual research conference, critical and scholarly Internet research independent from traditional disciplines and existing across academic borders.

ATLAS.ti   Software to support qualitative analysis of large bodies of textual, graphical, audio and video data.

Authenticity on the web   The extent to which material on the Internet is authentic, and how such authenticity can be assessed, is an ongoing issue. It relates to all Internet material from websites (e.g. determining if a site is a safe and credible location from which to trust its content or conduct Internet shopping) to social media personas (e.g. assessing whether a Twitter account is authored by a real person or a bot, namely a software application that runs automated tasks over the Internet).

Bank of England   The central bank of the UK which is owned by the UK government, and accountable to both Parliament and the general public.

Below-the-line sections   Comments posted online by readers in response to media texts where space is provided for this below the line of the original media article, for example, a news story or blog post. This space is a regular feature of many online news websites where such comments have replaced or supplemented traditional reader letters to the editor. Comments posted online may be moderated but, unlike letters to the editor, these below-the-line sections provide opportunities for reader debate as comments may be posted in response to other comments and not just the original media article.

Bespoke qualitative online research   Proprietary products offered by commercial organizations to collect qualitative data via Internet methods. Typically, these are products developed for organizations, particularly in the areas of market, consumer and opinion research. As such, they are not primarily designed for academic use and lack the flexibility of researcher-led methods of data collection.

Big data   Information from the Internet, for example, in the form of messages, updates and images posted to social networks, readings from sensors, signals from mobile devices and more. Many of the most important sources of big data (such as social media platforms) are relatively new. Big data is characterized not just by this variety but also by its volume (apparently more data now cross the Internet every second than were stored in the entire Internet 20 years ago) and its velocity (where speed of data creation enables the provision of real-time or nearly real-time information). The big data movement seeks to glean intelligence from data through analytics and to translate that into business advantage.

Blogs   A discussion or informational website published on the World Wide Web and consisting of discrete, often informal diary-style text entries known as posts.

Bounded episode   An occurrence of talk or text, such as a political speech or the publication of a report. Focused data in respect of this occurrence is selected for a limited time period to create a temporally and contextually bounded episode. An episode should have the potential to demonstrate its wider relevance through its analysis shedding light on wider societal issues. See also **discursive event**.

British Bankers Association   A trade association for the UK banking and financial services sector.

British Psychological Society (BPS)   A registered charity that acts as the representative body for psychology and psychologists in the UK. It is responsible for the promotion of excellence and ethical practice in the science, education and application of the discipline.

Building Societies Association   An association founded in the nineteenth century that represents all 43 UK building societies and the five large credit unions.

Cambridge Analytica   Cambridge Analytica Ltd was a British political consulting firm that combined data mining, data brokerage and data analysis with strategic communication during the electoral processes. The Facebook-Cambridge Analytica data scandal was a major political scandal in early 2018 when it was revealed that Cambridge Analytica had harvested the personal data from the Facebook profiles of millions of people without their consent and used it for political advertising purposes.

Computer assisted qualitative data analysis software (CAQDAS)   Specialist software that can assist researchers in the qualitative data analysis process. Such software can help with data organization and management, coding (including some automated coding), providing tools for commentary on the reflexive process of analysis, automated searching for words or phrases, generating word frequency searches and presenting material in different ways such as **mind maps** to help with ideas for analysis.

Confirming the research question   The process of testing and challenging the research question(s) for a piece of research. Most commonly this is undertaken by discussion with a research collaborator or supervisor through a review of a research proposal or comparison with the literature.

Construct   Within qualitative research, data are said to be constructed rather than collected to reflect the active processes of the researcher (and, if applicable, in interaction with the participant).

Content analysis   A method of data analysis that turns qualitative data into a format that can produce quantitative data in support of hypothesis testing or information gathering. Since a focus on counting means a loss in the richness that is typical in most qualitative data, a qualitative version of content analysis has been developed. This allows researchers to investigate a topic or phenomenon through a detailed examination and interpretation of data to detect patterns and themes.

Critical approaches   Research that questions the nature of reality and the ways in which we come to understand it, usually invoking a political aspect to scrutinize how our experiences are shaped.

Critical management studies   A movement grounded originally in a critical theory perspective that questions the authority and relevance of mainstream thinking and practice. Its focus is the field of management, business and organization where it critiques established social practices and institutional arrangements, challenges prevailing systems of domination and promotes the development of alternative ways of thinking.

Critical realism   A branch of philosophy that distinguishes between the 'real' world and the 'observable' world. The former cannot be observed and exists independent from human perceptions, theories and constructions. The world as we know and understand it is constructed from our perspectives and experiences, through what is 'observable'.

Curate   The management of data by the researcher during all stages of the research project in compliance with ethical and other regulatory principles.

Data sources   Specific locations (e.g. social media platforms) on the Internet from which data can be collected.

Data types   Forms of data on the Internet can be textual or visual, e.g. tweets, websites, blogs, Instagram postings, articles from news media (which might include stock images or cartoons), YouTube videos and Facebook pages.

Data variables   Different characteristics of Internet data such as language and country of origin.

Decentring of individual meaning   Whereas an interpretivist approach focuses on participants' meaning making, critical approaches displace this focus on the individual in favour of **deconstructing meaning**. See also **critical approaches** and **problematizing personal meaning**.

Deconstructing meaning   Deconstruction is a core process within the philosophical movement of post-structuralism. It involves dismantling preconceived ideas and showing what has been ignored in order to better understand both how a structure (such as how a word has come to have a particular meaning) has come to be built and its effects.

Dedoose   A cross-platform app for supporting analysis of qualitative and mixed methods research including text, photos, audio, videos and spreadsheet data.

Deepfake online videos   Computer-generated images of a subject's face created via analysis of thousands of still images of the person.

Device   A physical unit of equipment that contains a computer or microcontroller. Digital devices include smartphones, tablets and smartwatches.

Dialogic form   Relating to, or characterized by, dialogue and its use.

Digital ethnography   An online research method that adapts traditional ethnographic research methods to the study of the communities and cultures created through computer-mediated social interaction. See also **online ethnography**.

Digital methods   Research techniques made possible by the introduction of contemporary communication technologies. These methods study web-based activities and settings and use digital technologies to change some of the ways in which research is undertaken.

Dilemma of representation   The extent to which the researcher pays analytic attention to the individual who authors the online data that they are collecting and analysing. This will depend on the philosophical approach adopted in the research but also may be determined by whether the individual is already obscured (e.g. anonymous) by technological means or hyper-present (e.g. through a visible social media presence).

Discursive event   An approach within discourse analysis that creates a temporally and contextually bounded episode of talk or text. This is then analysed as a way of shedding light on a wider societal issue. See also **bounded episode**.

Discursive techniques   Methods of data analysis such as discourse analysis that draw on theories of discourse and social constructionism. These techniques pay attention to the significance and structuring effects of language and are concerned with identifying discourses and the processes of their social construction.

Discussion forums   Web-based electronic message boards on which people can post asynchronous communication, also commonly referred to as web forums, message boards or discussion boards. See also **discussion threads**.

Discussion threads   Asynchronous communications posted by people on web-based electronic message boards, also commonly referred to as web forums, message boards or discussion boards. See also **discussion forums**.

Economic & Social Research Council (ESRC)   The ESRC provides funding and support for research and training in the social sciences. It is part of UK Research and Innovation, a non-departmental public body funded by the UK government.

Emerald Publishing Guide   A series of 'How to' guides produced by Emerald Publishing for academic and practitioner authors. These contain practical tips and guidance on how to design, develop and present research.

Epistemological assumptions   Philosophical assumptions made about the way in which we understand and generate knowledge (what it is possible for us to know) and the ways in which knowledge claims can be asserted and defended (how we can obtain this knowledge).

Exchanges between individuals   See **discussion threads**.

Facebook   An online social media and social networking website that allows users to post comments, share photographs and post links to other web content.

Fake news   News, stories or hoaxes that are created to deliberately misinform or deceive readers. This deliberate disinformation can be spread both by traditional news media and online social media. These stories are often created to influence people's views, promote a political or social agenda or cause confusion.

FIFA Women's World Cup   An international football competition contested by the senior women's national teams of the members of *Fédération Internationale de Football Association* (FIFA), the sport's international governing body.

GIF   Standing for Graphical Interchange Format, a GIF is a series of images or soundless video that will loop continuously, can be embedded into social media and which does not require the user to press play.

Google Alerts   A content change detection and notification service offered by the search engine company Google. The service sends emails to the user when it finds new results on the Internet (for example, web pages, news items or blog posts) that match the user's search term(s).

Google image search   A search service owned by Google that allows users to search the World Wide Web for image content.

Grey literature   Material not published commercially or subject to the most rigorous standards of academic review. It can include reports and documents produced by many different types of organizations across the private, public and third sectors.

Grounded theory   A research method that is concerned with the development of theory from data which has been systematically collected and analysed. It is used to uncover such things as social relationships and behaviours of groups, known as social processes.

Hermeneutics   The theory and methodology of interpretation, especially the interpretation of philosophical texts.

HyperRESEARCH   Software to support qualitative research analysis.

Instagram   A photo and video-sharing social networking service that allows users to share photos and videos.

Internet Protocol (IP) address   The label that identifies a particular device on a network such as the Internet, similar to a post or zip code for a physical location. The

IP address is automatically assigned to every Internet-connected device via the software in its server/router.

Interpretivist   A philosophical approach in which research is concerned with accessing and understanding participants' intersubjective culturally derived meanings to explain behaviour. The object of research is the individual or collective experience of a particular aspect of reality.

Key actors   Individuals, groups or organizations who are likely to play the most significant role in relation to the chosen research topic.

Linguistic techniques   Methods of qualitative data analysis that focus on language and its use. These include narrative, template or thematic and rhetoric analysis.

Live streaming   Online streaming media that are simultaneously recorded and broadcast in real time. Live stream services include social media, video games and professional sports. These platforms often include the ability to talk to the broadcaster or participate in conversations in chat.

LSE Guide on Social Media Research   A series of blog posts that are part of the regularly updated Impact Blog hosted by the London School of Economics and Political Science. The blog features contributions from a range of writers interested in the impact of academic work in the social sciences and other disciplines.

Malware   This is malicious software that is harmful to a computer user such as computer viruses and spyware.

MAXQDA   A software package for qualitative and mixed methods research including but not limited to grounded theory, literature reviews, exploratory market research, qualitative text analyses and mixed methods approaches.

Meaning making   Where the research objective is to investigate the individual or collective experience (what it means to them) of a particular aspect of reality. See **interpretivist**.

Meme   An idea, behaviour or style that spreads from person to person within a culture (often on the Internet) and with the aim of conveying a particular phenomenon, theme or meaning.

Mind map   A diagram used to organize information visually. A mind map is hierarchical and shows relationships among components of the whole. Its structure radiates from the centre and can use lines, symbols, words, colour and images to organize the material.

Mode of access   This refers to how the researcher has accessed the Internet data they are collecting. Previous user activity on a device can shape how future web material is selected and presented so may differ depending on whether the researcher is using their own single use device, a device shared with a colleague or family member, or a public device.

Monitoring and revising the research question A reflexive process of ensuring that the focus and relevance of the research question is maintained throughout the research. See also **reflexivity**, **research diary**, **research training** and **snapshot**.

Multi-modal Where several modes (textual, aural, linguistic, spatial or visual) are used to create a single artifact; in the context of the Internet, this may include an element of interactivity.

Mumsnet A website for parents in the UK that hosts discussion forums where users share advice and information on parenting and other topics.

Netnography An approach to online research that was introduced in 1996 by Robert Kozinets in the fields of marketing and consumer research. It is a broad-based study of online social interaction and experience from a human perspective.

Numeric data Information about something that is measurable and is collected in number form.

NVivo Purpose-built software for qualitative and mixed methods research. It supports data organization, storage and retrieval; imports data from many sources (text, audio, video, emails, images, spreadsheets, online surveys, social and web content); and includes data management, query and visualization tools.

Online ethnography An online research method that adapts traditional ethnographic research methods to the study of the communities and cultures created through computer-mediated social interaction. See also **digital ethnography**.

Online identity A social identity that an Internet user establishes in online communities, email address, social media profile and websites. It can also be considered as an actively constructed presentation of oneself.

Ontological assumptions Philosophical assumptions about the nature of being which determine what we can know to be real (the nature of reality) and what we can know to exist.

Origin of access The physical location from which the researcher is accessing the Internet. See also **Internet protocol address**. This location determines factors such as the language and selection of material presented, for example, in web browsers. So, if the researcher uses the same digital device in two different countries, they will see different material in response to the same search in a web browser.

Phenomenology   The philosophical study of the structures of experience and consciousness.

Philosophical assumptions   See **epistemological assumptions** and **ontological assumptions**.

Platforms used   Digital services that facilitate interactions between two or more distinct but interdependent sets of users who interact through the service via the Internet. These include marketplaces (e.g. eBay), search engines (e.g. Google), social media (e.g. Facebook and Twitter) and communications services (e.g. Gmail).

Polyphonic   Producing or involving many voices.

Problematizing personal meaning   Research that focuses on the different forces and influences that shape the presentation (textual, visual, material) of different realities rather than seeking to discover what meaning this has to an individual or group of people.

Public documents   In the context of research ethics, documents that are in the public domain and which would not therefore require explicit informed consent from their author for them to be used as data in research.

QDA Miner   A qualitative data software package for coding, annotating, retrieving and analysing documents and images. It can be used to support analysis of texts, drawings, photographs, paintings and other types of visual documents.

Qualitative post-positivism   A meta-theoretical stance that critiques and amends positivism since it recognizes different framings of experience. Its underlying assumption is of real phenomena that can be accessed by objective qualitative research methods.

Qualitative research   Research that generates non-numeric data, which can be textual or visual, and which are **constructed** and **curated** through the research process. Qualitative research uses a wide range of methods developed from a variety of theoretical perspectives and underpinned by different philosophical stances. Often inductive and sometimes exploratory, such research is concerned with meanings, experiences, ideas and practices.

Realist   A philosophical approach to research which assumes that the objects of research are real phenomena that can be specified and discovered via the application of appropriately objective and scientific methods.

Reddit   An American social news aggregation, web content rating and discussion website.

Redundant items   Material that is identified through the data collection method but which turns out to be not relevant to the research question and which can be discarded as data.

Reflexivity The process of exercising critical thought in respect of one's own and the wider community of research practices. This awareness enables an understanding of both how knowledge is situated and the research and research community from which the knowledge has appeared.

Relativist A relativist perspective is a philosophical approach that challenges the notion of a 'concrete' reality and instead assumes that reality comes into being via various and complex processes of social construction.

Repeat items In the context of Internet data a repeat item is an item of data (such as a blogpost or news article) that has been published and collected in the dataset but which appears again, usually as a result of the original item being shared or liked in social media, in the alerts or other mechanism that is being used for data collection.

Research decisions The decision-making process in respect of all stages of the qualitative research project (e.g. what to include or exclude as data) and which should be documented by the researcher as part of an audit trail.

Research diary A reflexive written record of the researcher's activities, thoughts and feelings throughout the research process from design, data collection and analysis to writing up and presenting the study.

Research training In addition to providing specialist knowledge in relation to an aspect of research, attending such training may also provide an opportunity to share research or listen to others talking about their research and reflect these experiences back onto the research question.

Resources Material on different aspects of digital methods orientated to academic research.

Rogue websites These are sites set up for malicious or criminal purposes.

Saturation sample Data saturation is a concept used to refer to the point in data collection when no new information is being generated by additional data being collected and analysed. The term 'saturation sample' is used to indicate that sufficient data were collected in a research project to reach the point of saturation.

Selfie A self-portrait digital photograph, usually taken with a handheld smartphone and often shared on social media.

Snapshot As part of checking that the focus and relevance of the research question is maintained, a researcher might take a 'snapshot' of the material being collected and then review it. The snapshot might be a random selection of a fixed number of items of data or a single day's data collection. The researcher can use this data to record their initial reactions including the extent to which the data relates to the research question.

Snowballing technique   Adapted from a participant recruitment strategy, this technique involves following links in data identified during tracking and trawling methods in order to identify further relevant web data in relation to a specific research question.

Social Media Data Stewardship   Funded by Canada Research Chair, this is a research project applying the notion of data stewardship to social media data. The project focuses on studying the practices behind and attitudes towards the collection, storage, use, reuse, analysis, publishing and preservation of social media data.

Symbolic interactionism   An approach that focuses on the relationships among individuals within a society. This perspective sees people as being active in shaping the social world rather than simply being acted upon.

Tams Analyzer   An open source, Mac compatible coding and analysis program to support qualitative research.

Technological and platform variables   In the context of Internet research, these are the variables that the researcher needs to note as relevant to their understanding of the parameters of their research design.

Textual forms of communication   In the context of the Internet, these include blog posts, tweets, media articles and discussion forums. See **Discussion threads**.

Thematic analysis   A widely used analytic technique in business and management research. It entails a systematic approach to qualitative data that involves organizing usually textual data into themes. Themes, or patterns of cultural meaning, are generally a mix of top-down (pre-defined from the academic theory or empirical work) and bottom-up (the result of the researcher's interpretation of the data). Data are coded and classified by reference to these themes.

Threads of comments   See **discussion threads**.

Timeframes for data collection   The period during which data is collected. In a tracking methodology, this could be the time duration of running proprietary alerts; in a trawling methodology, this could be the time period for which Internet material is retrieved.

Tracking   A method of qualitative Internet data collection. Uses a variety of digital means (such as using proprietary tools) to track (or follow) a particular event and/or people or groups of interest and/or a concept due to their engagement with a specific topic of relevance to the research. It is usually prospective in that it involves tracking from the start of the project onwards in time to capture new material as it is published on the Internet.

Transana   Software to support analysis of primarily visual qualitative data including transcribing, categorizing and coding. The Professional version also handles text data.

Trawling   A method of qualitative Internet data collection. Uses specific key word search (such as in search engines) to provide potentially relevant material across a variety of source types (e.g. websites, blogs, Twitter). It is usually retrospective in that it involves trawling the Internet for existing material that has already been published or posted before the start of the research project.

Tumblr   A microblogging and social networking website that allows users to post multimedia and other content to a short-form blog.

Twitter   A microblogging and social networking service that allows users to post and interact with messages known as 'tweets' that are restricted to 280 characters.

UK Web Archive (UKWA)   A partnership of the six UK Legal Deposit Libraries, which collects millions of websites each year, preserving them for future generations. It performs an automated collection of UK websites at least once a year in order to capture as many websites as it can, which are curated on different topics and themes.

Visual analysis   A method by which visual images can be analysed as data. Examples include the use of visual portraiture codes, visual frame analysis, a visual semiotics approach and visual content analysis.

Visual digital data   Different forms of visual data found on the Internet including YouTube videos, photos, stock images and cartoons.

Visual forms of communication   In the context of the Internet, these include photographs, stock images, cartoons, pictures and videos. See also **GIF**.

WayBack Machine   A digital archive of the World Wide Web and other information on the Internet with free access to researchers, historians, scholars and the general public.

Yahoo   An American web services provider.

YouTube   A website that allows users to upload and share videos.

REFERENCES

Achievability (n.d.). Top 10 Software for Analysing Qualitative Data. Retrieved from www.achievability.co.uk/evasys/top-10-software-for-analysing-qualitative-data (accessed 2 July 2019).

Adams, R. J., Smart, P., and Huff, A. S. (2017). Shades of grey: Guidelines for working with the grey literature in systematic reviews for management and organizational studies. *International Journal of Management Reviews, 19*(4), 432-454.

Alvesson, M., and Deetz, S. (2000). *Doing Critical Management Research*. London: Sage.

Alvesson, M., and Skoldberg, K. (2000). *Reflexive Methodology: New Vistas for Qualitative Research*. London: Sage.

Atefeh, F., and Khreich, W. (2015). A survey of techniques for event detection in Twitter. *Computational Intelligence, 31*(1), 132-164.

Bachmann, D., and Elfrink, J. (1996). Tracking the progress of e-mail versus snail-mail. *Marketing Research, 8*(2), 31-35.

Baxter, G., and Marcella, R. (2017). Voters' online information behaviour and response to campaign content during the Scottish referendum on independence. *International Journal of Information Management, 37*(6), 539-546.

Bell, E., and Leonard, P. (2018). Digital organizational storytelling on YouTube: Constructing plausibility through network protocols of amateurism, affinity, and authenticity. *Journal of Management Inquiry, 27*(3), 339-351.

Bellemare, A. (2019). The real 'fake news': How to spot misinformation and disinformation online, *CBC News*, 4 July.

Benschop, Y., and Meihuizen, H. E. (2002). Keeping up gendered appearances: representations of gender in financial annual reports. *Accounting Organizations and Society, 27*(7), 611-636.

Billig, M. (2001). Humour and hatred: The racist jokes of the Ku Klux Klan. *Discourse & Society, 12*(3), 267-289.

Boje, D., and Smith, R. (2010). Re-storying and visualizing the changing entrepreneurial identities of Bill Gates and Richard Branson. *Culture and Organization, 16*(4), 307-331.

Boland, T. (2016). Seeking a role: Disciplining jobseekers as actors in the labour market. *Work Employment and Society, 30*(2), 334-351.

Breitbarth, T., Harris, P., and Insch, A. (2010). Pictures at an exhibition revisited: Reflections on a typology of images used in the construction of corporate social responsibility and sustainability in non-financial corporate reporting. *Journal of Public Affairs, 10*(4), 238-257.

British Psychological Society (2007). *Report of the Working Party on Conducting Research on the Internet: Guidelines for Ethical Practice in Psychological Research Online*. Leicester: British Psychological Society.

British Psychological Society (2009). *Code of Ethics and Conduct: Guidance Published by the Ethics Committee of the BPS*. Leicester: British Psychological Society.

British Psychological Society (2014). *Code of Human Research Ethics* (Vol. INF180/12.2014). Leicester: British Psychological Society.

British Psychological Society (2017). *Ethics Guidelines for Internet-mediated Research* (Vol. INF206/04.2017). Leicester: British Psychological Society.

Burnap, P., Rana, O. F., Avis, N., Williams, M., Housley, W., Edwards, A., Morgan, J., and Sloan, L. (2015). Detecting tension in online communities with computational Twitter analysis. *Technological Forecasting and Social Change, 95*, 96-108.

Cassell, C. (2015). *Conducting Research Interviews for Business and Management Students*. London: Sage.

Cassell, C., and Symon, G. (2011). Assessing 'good' qualitative research in the work psychology field: A narrative analysis. *Journal of Occupational and Organizational Psychology, 84*(4), 633-650.

Chang-Kredl, S., and Colannino, D. (2017). Constructing the image of the teacher on Reddit: Best and worst teachers. *Teaching and Teacher Education, 64*(C), 43-51.

Chivers, T. (2019). What do we do about the deepfake video? *The Guardian*, 23 June.

Cohen-Almagor, R. (2011). Internet history. *International Journal of Technoethics, 2*(2), 45-64.

Cordoba-Pachon, J. R., and Loureiro-Koechlin, C. (2015). Online ethnography: A study of software developers and software development. *Baltic Journal of Management, 10*(2), 188-202.

Coupland, C. (2005). Corporate social responsibility as argument on the web. *Journal of Business Ethics, 62*(4), 355-366.

Coupland, C., and Brown, A. D. (2004). Constructing organizational identities on the web: A case study of Royal Dutch/Shell. *Journal of Management Studies, 41*(8), 1325-1347.

Davison, J. (2010). [In]visible [in]tangibles: Visual portraits of the business elite. *Accounting Organizations and Society, 35*(2), 165-183.

Delmestri, G., Oberg, A., and Drori, G. S. (2015). The unbearable lightness of university branding. *International Studies of Management & Organization, 45*(2), 121-136.

Denzin, N. K., and Lincoln, Y. S. (eds) (1994). *Handbook of Qualitative Research.* Thousand Oaks, CA and London: Sage.

Duberley, J., Johnson, P., and Cassell, C. (2012). Philosophies underpinning qualitative research. In G. Symon and C. Cassell (eds), *Qualitative Organizational Research: Core Methods and Current Challenges* (pp. 15-34). London: Sage.

Duff, A. (2011). Big four accounting firms' annual reviews: A photo analysis of gender and race portrayals. *Critical Perspectives on Accounting, 22*(1), 20-38.

Duffy, B. E., and Hund, E. (2015). 'Having it all' on social media: Entrepreneurial femininity and self-branding among fashion bloggers. *Social Media + Society, 1*(2).

Dutton, W. H. (2013). *The Oxford Handbook of Internet Studies.* Oxford: Oxford University Press.

Easterby-Smith, M., Golden-Biddle, K., and Locke, K. (2008). Working with pluralism: Determining quality in qualitative research. *Organizational Research Methods, 11*(3), 419-429.

Eberle, T. (2014). Phenomenology as a research method. In U. Flick (ed.), *The SAGE Handbook of Qualitative Data Analysis* (pp. 184-202). London: Sage.

Eriksson, P., and Kovalainen, A. (2015). *Qualitative Methods in Business Research: A Practical Guide to Social Research.* London: Sage.

ESRC (2015). *ESRC Framework for Research Ethics.* Updated January 2015. Swindon: Economic & Social Research Council.

Ess, C. (2009). *Digital Media Ethics.* Cambridge: Polity.

Eysenbach, G., and Till, J. E. (2001). Ethical issues in qualitative research on Internet communities. *British Medical Journal, 323*(7321), 1103-1105.

Fahmy, S., Kelly, J., and Kim, Y. S. (2007). What Katrina revealed: A visual analysis of the hurricane coverage by news wires and U.S. newspapers. *Journalism & Mass Communication Quarterly, 84*(3), 546-561.

Fielding, N., Lee, R. M., and Blank, G. (2008). The Internet as a research medium: An editorial introduction to the SAGE Handbook of Online Research Methods. In N. Fielding, R. M. Lee and G. Blank (eds), *The SAGE Handbook of Online Research Methods* (pp. 3-20). Los Angeles and London: Sage.

Francis, J. J., Johnston, M., Robertson, C., Glidewell, L., Entwistle, V., Eccles, M. P., and Grimshaw, J. M. (2010). What is an adequate sample size? Operationalising data saturation for theory-based interview studies. *Psychology & Health, 25*(10), 1229-1245.

Glozer, S., Caruana, R., and Hibbert, S. A. (2019). The never-ending story: Discursive legitimation in social media dialogue. *Organization Studies, 40*(5), 625-650.

Hardy, C., and Maguire, S. (2010). Discourse, field-configuring events, and change in organizations and institutional fields: Narratives of DDT and the Stockholm Convention. *Academy of Management Journal, 53*(6), 1365-1392.

Hardy, C., Phillips, N., and Clegg, S. R. (2001). Reflexivity in organization and manage-ment theory: A study of the production of the research 'subject'. *Human Relations, 54*(5), 531–560.

Highfield, T., and Leaver, T. (2016). Instagrammatics and digital methods: studying visual social media, from selfies and GIFs to memes and emoji. *Communication Research and Practice, 2*(1), 47–62.

Hinchcliffe, V., and Gavin, H. (2009). Social and virtual networks: Evaluating synchro-nous online interviewing using Instant Messenger. *The Qualitative Report, 14*(2), 318–340.

Hine, C. (2005). Internet research and the sociology of cyber-social-scientific knowl-edge. *The Information Society, 21*, 239–248.

Hine, C. (2008). Virtual ethnography: Modes, varieties, affordances. In N. Fielding, R. M. Lee and G. Blank (eds), *The SAGE Handbook of Online Research Methods* (pp. 257–270). Los Angeles and London: Sage.

Hine, C. (2012). *The Internet: Understanding Qualitative Research*. New York and Oxford: Oxford University Press.

Hine, C. (ed.) (2013). *Virtual Research Methods*. London: Sage.

Hine, C. (2014). Headlice eradication as everyday engagement with science: An analysis of online parenting discussions. *Public Understanding of Science, 23*(5), 574–591.

Höllerer, M. A. (2013). From taken-for-granted to explicit commitment: The rise of CSR in a corporatist country. *Journal of Management Studies, 50*(4), 573–606.

Janghorban, R., Roudsari, R. L., and Taghipour, A. (2014). Skype interviewing: The new generation of online synchronous interview in qualitative research. *International Journal of Qualitative Studies on Health and Well-Being, 9*, https://doi.org/10.3402/qhw.v9.24152.

Karpf, D. (2012). Social science research methods in Internet time. *Information Communication & Society, 15*(5), 639–661.

Kassinis, G., and Panayiotou, A. (2017). Website stories in times of distress. *Management Learning, 48*(4), 397–415.

Kelly, J., Fealy, G. M., and Watson, R. (2012). The image of you: Constructing nursing identities in YouTube. *Journal of Advanced Nursing, 68*(8), 1804–1813.

Kiesler, S. (2014). *Culture of the Internet*. New York: Psychology Press.

Kozinets, R. V. (2010). *Netnography: Doing Ethnographic Research Online*. London: Sage.

Kozinets, R. V. (2019). *Netnography: The Essential Guide to Qualitative Social Media Research* (3rd edn). London: Sage.

Kozinets, R. V., Dolbec, P., and Earley, A. (2014). Netnographic Analysis: Understanding Culture through Social Media Data. In U. Flick (ed.), *SAGE Handbook of Qualitative Data Analysis* (pp. 262–275). London: Sage.

Kress, G., and van Leeuwen, T. (1996). *Reading Images: The Grammar of Visual Design*. London: Routledge.

Lazer, D. M. J., Baum, M. A., Benkler, Y., Berinsky, A. J., Greenhill, K. M., Menczer, F., Metzger, M. J., Nyhan, B., Pennycook, G., Rothschild, D., Schudson, M., Sloman, S. A., Sunstein, C. R., Thorson, E. A., Watts, D. J., and Zittrain, J. L. (2018). The science of fake news. *Science, 359*(6380), 1094–1096.

Lee, B. (2012). Using documents in organizational research. In G. Symon and C. Cassell (eds), *Qualitative Organizational Research: Core Methods and Current Challenges* (pp. 389–407). London: Sage.

Lemke, J. L. (1999). Discourse and organizational dynamics: Website communication and institutional change. *Discourse & Society, 10*(1), 21–47.

Lillqvist, E., Moisander, J. K., and Firat, A. F. (2018). Consumers as legitimating agents: How consumer-citizens challenge marketer legitimacy on social media. *International Journal of Consumer Studies, 42*(2), 197–204.

Markham, A. (2010). Internet research. In D. Silverman (ed.), *Qualitative Research: Issues of Theory, Method and Practice* (3rd edn). London: Sage.

Markham, A., and Buchanan, E. (2012). *Ethical Decision-Making and Internet Research: Recommendations from the AoIR Ethics Working Committee* (Version 2.0). Association of Internet Researchers. Retrieved from: https://aoir.org/reports/ethics2.pdf (accessed 6 July 2020).

Mason, J. (2002). *Qualitative Researching* (2nd edn). London: Sage.

Mescher, S., Benschop, Y., and Doorewaard, H. (2010). Representations of work-life balance support. *Human Relations, 63*(1), 21–39.

Meyer, R. E., Hollerer, M. A., Jancsary, D., and Van Leeuwen, T. (2013). The visual dimension in organizing, organization, and organization research: Core ideas, current developments, and promising avenues. *Academy of Management Annals, 7*(1), 489–555.

Milner, R. M. (2016). *The World Made Meme: Public Conversations and Participatory Media*. Cambridge, MA: MIT Press.

Miltner, K. M., and Highfield, T. (2017). Never gonna GIF you up: Analyzing the cultural significance of the animated GIF. *Social Media + Society, 3*(3), https://doi.org/10.1177/2056305117725223.

Mollett, A., Moran, D., and Dunleavy, P. (2011). *Using Twitter in University Research, Teaching and Impact Activities*. Impact of social sciences: Maximizing the impact of academic research. LSE Public Policy Group. London: London School of Economics and Political Science.

Monson, O., Donaghue, N., and Gill, R. (2016). Working hard on the outside: A multimodal critical discourse analysis of The Biggest Loser Australia. *Social Semiotics, 26*(5), 524–540.

Moor, L., and Kanji, S. (2019). Money and relationships online: Communication and norm formation in women's discussions of couple resource allocation. *The British Journal of Sociology, 70*(3), 948–968.

Morton, A. (1977). *A Guide Through the Theory of Knowledge*. Oxford: Blackwell.

Murthy, D. (2008). Digital ethnography: An examination of the use of new technologies for social research. *Sociology – the Journal of the British Sociological Association, 42*(5), 837–855.

Oates, C. J., and Alevizou, P. J. (2017). *Conducting Focus Groups for Business and Management Students*. London: Sage.

Oddo, J. (2013). Precontextualization and the rhetoric of futurity: Foretelling Colin Powell's UN address on NBC News. *Discourse & Communication*, 7(1), 25-53.

O'Reilly, M., and Parker, N. (2013). 'Unsatisfactory saturation': A critical exploration of the notion of saturated sample sizes in qualitative research. *Qualitative Research*, 13(2), 190-197.

Orlikowski, W. J., and Scott, S. V. (2014). What happens when evaluation goes online? Exploring apparatuses of valuation in the travel sector. *Organization Science*, 25(3), 868-891.

Ozdora-Aksak, E., and Atakan-Duman, S. (2015). The online presence of Turkish banks: Communicating the softer side of corporate identity. *Public Relations Review*, 41(1), 119-128.

Pablo, Z., and Hardy, C. (2009). Merging, masquerading and morphing: Metaphors and the World Wide Web. *Organization Studies*, 30(8), 821-843.

Palfrey, J. (2010). Four phases of Internet regulation. *Social Research*, 77(3), 981-996.

Pearce, W., Özkula, S. M., Greene, A. K., Teeling, L., Bansard, J. S., Omena, J. J., and Rabello, E. T. (2018). Visual cross-platform analysis: Digital methods to research social media images. *Information, Communication & Society*, 1-20.

Perren, L., and Jennings, P. L. (2005). Government discourses on entrepreneurship: Issues of legitimization, subjugation, and power. *Entrepreneurship Theory and Practice*, 29(2), 173-184.

Phillips, N., and Hardy, C. (2002). *Discourse Analysis: Investigating Processes of Social Construction*. London: Sage.

Pittenger, D. J. (2003). Internet research: An opportunity to revisit classic ethical problems in behavioral research. *Ethics & Behavior*, 13(1), 45-60.

Pritchard, K. (2020). Examining web images: A Combined Visual Analysis (CVA) approach. *European Management Review*, 17(1), 297-310.

Pritchard, K., and Whiting, R. (2012a). Autopilot? A reflexive review of the piloting process in qualitative e-research. *Qualitative Research in Organizations and Management*, 7(3), 338-353.

Pritchard, K., and Whiting, R. (2012b). *Tracking and trawling: Theorising 'participants' and 'data' in qualitative e-research*. Paper presented at the British Academy of Management Annual Conference, Cardiff.

Pritchard, K., and Whiting, R. (2014). Baby Boomers and the lost generation: On the discursive construction of generations at work. *Organization Studies*, 35(11), 1605-1626.

Pritchard, K., and Whiting, R. (2015). Taking stock: A visual analysis of gendered ageing. *Gender, Work & Organization*, 22(5), 510-528.

Pritchard, K., and Whiting, R. (2017). Analysing web images. In C. Cassell, A. L. Cunliffe and G. Grandy (eds), *The SAGE Handbook of Qualitative Business and Management Research Methods* (Vol. 2, pp. 282-297). London: Sage.

Rhodes, C. (2009). After reflexivity: Ethics, freedom and the writing of organization studies. *Organization Studies, 30*(6), 653–672.

Richards, L. (2009). *Handling Qualitative Data: A Practical Guide* (2nd edn). London: Sage.

Rindova, V. P., and Kotha, S. (2001). Continuous 'morphing': Competing through dynamic capabilities, form, and function. *Academy of Management Journal, 44*(6), 1263–1280.

Rokka, J., and Canniford, R. (2016). Heterotopian selfies: How social media destabilizes brand assemblages. *European Journal of Marketing, 50*(9/10), 1789–1813.

Rose, G. (2012). *Visual Methodologies: An Introduction to Researching with Visual Materials* (3rd edn). London: Sage.

Rothaermel, F. T., and Sugiyama, S. (2001). Virtual Internet communities and commercial success: Individual and community-level theory grounded in the atypical case of TimeZone.com. *Journal of Management, 27*(3), 297–312.

Saunders, B., Sim, J., Kingstone, T., Baker, S., Waterfield, J., Bartlam, B., Burroughs, H., and Jinks, C. (2018). Saturation in qualitative research: Exploring its conceptualization and operationalization. *Quality & Quantity, 52*(4), 1893–1907.

Saunders, M. N. K., and Townsend, K. (2018). Choosing participants. In C. Cassell, A. Cunliffe and G. Grandy (eds), *The SAGE Handbook of Qualitative Business and Management Research Methods* (pp. 480–494). London: Sage.

Schultze, U., and Mason, R. O. (2012). Studying cyborgs: Re-examining Internet studies as human subjects research. *Journal of Information Technology, 27*(4), 301–312.

Shifman, L. (2012). An anatomy of a YouTube meme. *New Media & Society, 14*(2), 187–203.

Sillince, J. A. A., and Brown, A. D. (2009). Multiple organizational identities and legitimacy: The rhetoric of police websites. *Human Relations, 62*(12), 1829–1856.

Simsek, Z., and Veiga, J. F. (2001). A primer on Internet organizational surveys. *Organizational Research Methods, 4*(3), 218–235.

Singh, V., and Point, S. (2006). (Re)presentations of gender and ethnicity in diversity statements on European company websites. *Journal of Business Ethics, 68*(4), 363–379.

Snelson, C. L. (2016). Qualitative and mixed methods social media research: A review of the literature. *International Journal of Qualitative Methods, 15*(1), https://doi.org/10.1177/1609406915624574.

Sproull, L., Dutton, W., and Kiesler, S. (2007). Introduction to the special issue: Online communities. *Organization Studies, 28*(3), 277–281.

Stablein, R. (2006). Data in organization studies. In S. Clegg, C. Hardy, W. Nord and T. B. Lawrence (eds), *The SAGE Handbook of Organization Studies* (pp. 347–369). London: Sage.

Stewart, D. R. C., and Littau, J. (2016). Up, Periscope: Mobile streaming video technologies, privacy in public, and the right to record. *Journalism & Mass Communication Quarterly, 93*(2), 312–331.

Stoycheff, E., Liu, J., Wibowo, K. A., and Nanni, D. P. (2017). What have we learned about social media by studying Facebook? A decade in review. *New Media & Society, 19*(6), 968–980.

Sundstrom, B., and Levenshus, A. B. (2017). The art of engagement: Dialogic strategies on Twitter. *Journal of Communication Management, 21*(1), 17–33.

Swan, E. (2017). Postfeminist stylistics, work femininities and coaching: A multimodal study of a website. *Gender Work and Organization, 24*(3), 274–296.

Symon, G., and Cassell, C. (2016). Qualitative I-O psychology: A view from Europe. *Industrial and Organizational Psychology-Perspectives on Science and Practice, 9*(4), 744–747.

Symon, G., Cassell, C., and Johnson, P. (2018). Evaluative practices in qualitative management research: A critical review. *International Journal of Management Reviews, 20*(1), 134–154.

Thompson, L. F., Surface, E. A., Martin, D. L., and Sanders, M. G. (2003). From paper to pixels: Moving personnel surveys to the web. *Personnel Psychology, 56*(1), 197–227.

Thurlow, A. (2018). *Social Media, Organizational Identity and Public Relations: The Challenge of Authenticity*. Abingdon: Routledge.

Townsend, L., and Wallace, C. (2016). *Social Media Research: A Guide to Ethics*. Aberdeen: University of Aberdeen. Retrieved from: www.gla.ac.uk/media/media_487729_en.pdf (accessed 22 June 2020).

Travers, M. (2009). New methods, old problems: A sceptical view of innovation in qualitative research. *Qualitative Research, 9*(2), 161–179.

van Bommel, K., and Spicer, A. (2011). Hail the snail: Hegemonic struggles in the Slow Food movement. *Organization Studies, 32*(12), 1717–1744.

Wasim, A. (2019). *Using Twitter as a data source: An overview of social media research tools*. Retrieved from: https://blogs.lse.ac.uk/impactofsocialsciences/2019/06/18/using-twitter-as-a-data-source-an-overview-of-social-media-research-tools-2019/ (accessed 22 June 2020).

Waters, R. D., Burnett, E., Lamm, A., and Lucas, J. (2009). Engaging stakeholders through social networking: How nonprofit organizations are using Facebook. *Public Relations Review, 35*(2), 102–106.

Wernet, A. (2014). Hermeneutics and objective hermeneutics. In U. Flick (ed.), *The SAGE Handbook of Qualitative Data Analysis* (pp. 234–246). London: Sage.

Whiting, R., and Pritchard, K. (2017). Digital ethics. In C. Cassell, A. L. Cunliffe and G. Grandy (eds), *The SAGE Handbook of Qualitative Business and Management Research Methods* (Vol. 1, pp. 562–579). London: Sage.

Whiting, R., and Pritchard, K. (2020). Reconstructing retirement as an enterprising endeavor. *Journal of Management Inquiry, 29*(4), 404–417.

Whiting, R., and Pritchard, K. (2019). *Weary women? The responsibility for gendered representations of retirement*. Paper presented at the European Group for Organizational Studies conference, Edinburgh, July.

Yanow, D., and Tsoukas, H. (2009). What is reflection-in-action? A phenomenological account. *Journal of Management Studies, 46*(8), 1339–1364.

Yun, G. W., and Trumbo, C. W. (2000). Comparative response to a survey executed by post, e-mail, & web form. *Journal of Computer-Mediated Communication,* 6(1), https://doi.org/10.1111/j.1083-6101.2000.tb00112.x.

INDEX

Fold a Rabbit

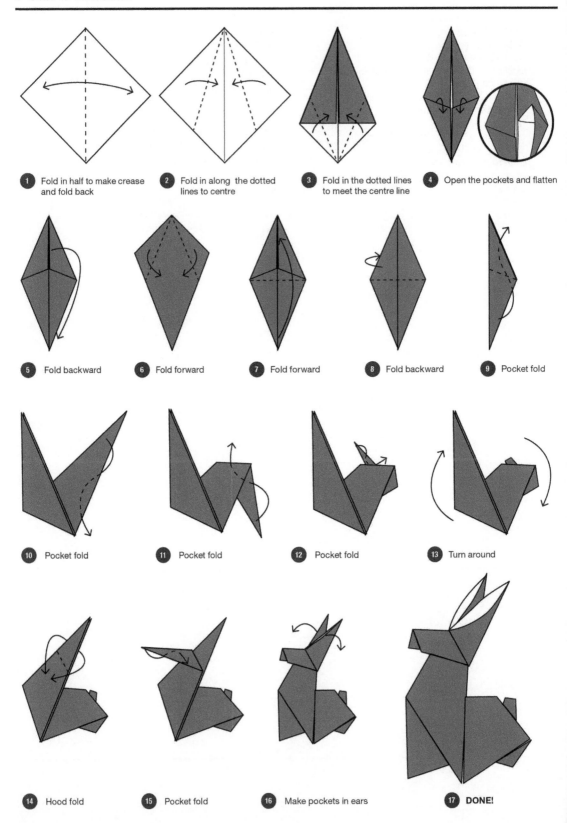

1. Fold in half to make crease and fold back
2. Fold in along the dotted lines to centre
3. Fold in the dotted lines to meet the centre line
4. Open the pockets and flatten
5. Fold backward
6. Fold forward
7. Fold forward
8. Fold backward
9. Pocket fold
10. Pocket fold
11. Pocket fold
12. Pocket fold
13. Turn around
14. Hood fold
15. Pocket fold
16. Make pockets in ears
17. DONE!